rhododendrons
camellias and magnolias
2008

Royal
Horticultural
Society

Published in 2008 by
the Royal Horticultural Society,
80 Vincent Square, London SW1P 2PE

ISBN 978 1 902896 85 4

Designed for the RHS by Sharon Cluett

Edited for the RHS by Simon Maughan

Honorary Editor for the Rhododendron,
Camellia and Magnolia Group
Pam Hayward

Printed by MPG Books Ltd, Bodmin, Cornwall

COVER ILLLUSTRATIONS
FRONT COVER: *Magnolia lotungensis*
(Zeng Qing-Wen)
BACK COVER (TOP): *Rhododendron
loranthiflorum* (Michael Shuttleworth)
BACK COVER (BOTTOM): *Camellia 'Wildfire'*
(Michael Shuttleworth)

Royal
Horticultural
Society

Contents

Chairman's foreword   5
MIKE ROBINSON

Editorial   7
PAM HAYWARD

Random hybrid thoughts   9
GEOFF TAYLOR

Finding Mr Wilson   14
MARK FLANAGAN

Wilson study day 2007   24
MIKE ROBINSON

Evaluation of cold hardiness and
ornamental characteristics of Korean
provenances of *Camellia japonica*   26
ANTHONY S AIELLO, ELINOR I GOFF,
SHELLEY DILLARD & MICHELLE CONNERS

Francis Hanger – the father of
modern rhododenron breeding   32
COLIN CROSBIE

The threat of *Phytophthora ramorum*
to woody plant collections...   35
IAN WRIGHT

Kalmias – American Beauties   43
ALAN PULLEN

Magnolia sargentiana and *Magnolia
dawsoniana*: Exploration and field
surveys in the Dafengding of
southern Sichuan   50
PETER WHARTON

Breeding evergreen azaleas
at Glendoick   59
KENNETH COX

Arduaine Garden, Argyll: An historical
perspective   64
JOHN M HAMMOND

Who do you grow?   76
MALCOLM NASH

Notes on the cultivation, morphology
and nomenclature of eleven hardy
Asian evergreen magnolias   81
RICHARD B FIGLAR

New evergreen magnolias:
Comments from UK growers   94
MIKE ROBINSON, JOHN MARSTON & MAURICE FOSTER

Rhododendron conservation
at Nymans   97
ED IKIN

Current taxonomy – *Rhododendron
vanderbiltianum* MERR.   100
GEORGE ARGENT, MICHAEL MÖLLER & ALEXANDRA CLARK

Children of Chance – breeding
camellias   104
NICK CREEK

Warren Berg – a personal tribute   107
STEVE HOOTMAN

Book review   111
The Rhododendrons of Sabah, Malaysian Borneo
CHRIS CALLARD

Exceptional plants 2007   113
Exceptional new hybrids 2007   118
Awards to plants 2006/2007   120
Challenge Cup winners   124

RHS Rhododendron and Camellia
Committee   127

Rhododendron, Camellia & Magnolia
Group   128

Index   130

Chairman's Foreword

MIKE ROBINSON

'Nothing is worth doing unless it is worth doing badly'   OSCAR WILDE

The big RHS shows continue to attract vast numbers of visitors, with Chelsea still one of the opening events of the London 'season.' The floral displays in the marquee are spectacular, and it is nice to see space given to the plants that received awards from the plant committees on the Monday morning.

I wonder, though, if I am alone in finding so many of the show gardens unreal? Beautiful as most of them are, with not a dead leaf in sight, and with superb water and hard landscaping features, the best are, indeed, works of art. However, aren't they about as much help to the average gardener as a designer dress is to the woman (I hope I am sufficiently politically correct) on the Clapham omnibus: perfection but unattainable?

Of necessity a show garden is a snapshot in time and must be judged as such, in the same way as a painting is judged next to the landscape it portrays. The latter, however, is continually changing. So it is with a show garden: it is impossible for it to display development and growth.

Let us therefore imagine how a real garden might develop from the beginning. Often, after an interval spent clearing weeds and unwanted trees, modifying the mistakes of the last owner, and getting the place presentable, many of us become enthusiastic about particular genera; there cannot be many who, after a few years gardening, do not have one or more favourites (or obsessions). This frequently leads to a campaign to collect the best varieties by visiting specialist nurseries instead of the local garden centre, reading the literature, and even by joining a specialist group! To fit in all the rare gems, planting often tends to be too close and

may well lack any long term planning, perhaps grouping related species and hybrids rather than considering the overall effect.

Sooner or later, plants with the collectors' numbers on their labels arrive: this leads to that most virulent infection – the wish to have the latest and best introductions from the wild. From there follows the highly desirable concern for wild habitats, the gathering of knowledge about countries of origin and the way local people use plants – leading to a broadening interest in diverse cultures, ecology, climatic variation and plant sciences. It has been, in my own case, only then that a consideration of hard landscaping, seasonal and colour combinations has begun – in short – a requirement for design. My garden has given an enormous amount of pleasure to us all, but really was 'done badly'. It has always been, and still is, the plants first.

This is not to denigrate the profession of garden design, but one has to have considerable resources, or a very small garden, to start out by engaging a first rate professional. It is perhaps not unfair to suggest, for example, that the Chelsea show garden is designed to attract primarily the urban dwelling professional. My only criticism is that in this concentration on design at RHS shows, the love of plants and the study of their origins have been lost, so that the evolution I have described and which I believe happens in the majority of gardens is too little considered at present. Visiting friends' gardens and watching their development to maturity has been, for me, by far the biggest influence. Gardens and plants do, after all, grow!

How they have grown this year! Never before have I been so conscious of the amount of growth on established woody plants: rhododendrons, camellias, berberis, roses, deutzias and so on, with the *victor ludorum* here going to magnolias: extension growth of over a metre on small trees has been common, and two metres was achieved by a small graft

CAMELLIA 'Browncreek's Chiffon'
MICHAEL SHUTTLEWORTH

of *M.* 'Royal Alma'– one of Ian Baldick's New Zealand hybrids.

Of course the magnitude of this year's growth has, yet again, reminded me that I have planted too close. I have spent more time pruning and removing the less satisfactory performers than planting this season.

However, it has been great fun making mistakes instead of starting with perfection, which would never be attained anyway. It is the asymptotic pursuit of perfection and the continually renewed challenge this presents that provides most of the pleasure. I shall continue to underestimate the rate of growth of new acquisitions, and to put things in the wrong place. Perhaps I should have given more thought to the overall design initially – or perhaps not – collecting too many varieties has maintained my enthusiasm, and brought me into contact with so many generous and friendly people and so many exquisite plants.

It is the very different weather from that of 2006 that has caused such growth in the southeast of England: little sunshine, few high temperatures, low light levels and very much more rain. In spite of this, the bud set on magnolias is excellent for the fourth year running, and I hear similar reports of rhododendrons and camellias from all over the country. One must hope, with so much unripened wood around on marginally hardy plants, that the long predicted harsh winter does not come to pass.

Once more Nature has confounded those foolish enough to forecast anything but a few days ahead or, perhaps, the longest term trends. She has averaged things out to great benefit by following a hot dry summer with a cold wet one: almost all those poor parched things of 2006 have more than recovered from their pathetic appearance after the drought.

Pam Hayward, in her first year as editor, has collected together an altogether elegant selection of variety and quality: we continue tradition by having a yearbook bursting with enthusiasm for plants! I hope you all enjoy it.

Editorial

PAM HAYWARD

To become Editor of the yearbook of the Rhododendron, Camellia and Magnolia Group is a privilege; to take it on from here is a considerable responsibility. In recent years the publication has built on a deserved reputation of 60 years by maintaining the acknowledged high standard of contributions whilst embracing those elements of new technology which can enhance the content.

It is my ambition to see that trend continue and to steer a course which keeps the yearbook at the centre of current debate while recognising and drawing upon our rich heritage, retaining an intelligent stance which informs and challenges our membership, yet remains an entertaining and enjoyable read.

Threats to the survival of our plants and gardens come in many guises, from the extremes of war, disease and weather events to the gentler decline and neglect brought about by the vagaries of fashion or fortune. Time alone has led to so many of our plants or the people associated with them being forgotten, and failure to properly record or propagate and distribute plants accounts for even more of our 'missing'.

The impact of *Phytophthora ramorum*, the Great Storm of 1987 and the changing fortunes of the garden at Arduaine, described in this edition, are timely reminders of just how fragile our planted heritage is and how vital it is that we address ourselves responsibly to its proper care.

The *Red List of the Magnoliaceae*, published in 2007, graphically outlines the threat to our natural environment, from which we, as collectors and growers of our three great genera, have drawn for decades. Peter Wharton travelled to southern Sichuan to examine the impact deforestation has had on *Magnolia sargentiana* and *M. dawsoniana*. His fascinating account is ultimately optimistic and demonstrates that regeneration can be a reality when practical conservation measures are implemented.

More reassuring still is Mark Flanagan's wonderful description of his inspired visit to Sichuan in the footsteps of the great plant hunter Ernest Henry Wilson, which highlights how little the landscape has altered since Wilson's trips in the early years of last century. This seems remarkable when viewed against the constant and pessimistic images we now have of China's development 'juggernaut'.

Recognising these threats should help us value new introductions and varieties all the more, and the opportunity to grow a whole new range of evergreen magnolias, afforded by the effects of climate change, is an excellent starting point. Richard Figlar describes eleven Asian species which are becoming suitable candidates for our more temperate conditions, potential which is confirmed and reinforced by the experiences of three eminent magnolia growers in the UK.

Pushing the boundaries of what can be cultivated is also happening in the camellia world: a 20 year study at the Morris Arboretum gives hope to those still unfortunate enough to be unable to grow *Camellia japonica* unprotected.

Raising new varieties is a passion common to all plant enthusiasts; hybridising is serious business…or is it? Certainly for Kenneth Cox, a profound desire to address the commonly perceived low opinion of the evergreen azalea in the UK has led him on a dedicated mission to produce a range of varieties destined to become much more than 'fillers' and 'landscaping' material. For Geoff Taylor, however, recollections of rhododendron hybridising over almost 50 years reveal the sheer fun and pleasure to be had – from the contemplation of suitable parentage right through to the selection of names for the chosen few. The self-effacing Nick Creek has his eye on the show bench as he harnesses 'chance' and no small measure of skill to produce winning camellia varieties.

One of the recurring themes in recent yearbooks has been the desirability of complementing and extending our garden displays by incorporating other genera. Kalmias offer another beautiful addition to our palette, flowering after the main rhododendron hybrid display, just as the deciduous azaleas have peaked, and before the hydrangeas. Alan Pullen, custodian of the National Collection of Kalmias, provides an enticing invitation to include them in our gardens.

Two outstanding individuals are celebrated in this edition – Warren Berg, renowned world-wide as a discerning rhododendron collector and talented hybridiser, and Francis Hanger, whose legacy as the 'father of modern rhododendron breeding' has languished unsung for 45 years.

After years of inclusion in the yearbook, it was felt sensible to publish the detailed show and tour reports in the Bulletin where they will appear when the events are fresh in the memory and have more relevance. However, the major show awards and exceptional plants seen at shows, on tours and on offer from our nurserymen will be recorded in the yearbook, together with plants receiving awards.

It is hoped this offering has something of interest to all Group members and that the new design is favourably received.

Finally, I must express thanks both to my predecessor, Philip Evans, for his help and support, and to the contributors who, without exception, have been a pleasure to work with and from whom I have learned a great deal.

Random hybrid thoughts

GEOFF TAYLOR

WHEN THERE ARE SO MANY rhododendrons on the Register, why hybridize more? Replacement of valuable crosses lost to cultivation, the employment of little used species, later flowering among the dwarfs, introduction of colour to those blooming in July and the possibility of repeat flowering via the *Vireya* subgenus; these are all projects for the dedicated amateur.

Nearly half a century ago, I began crossing rhododendrons merely for fun. Seeking new colour breaks, I crossed *Rhododendron augustinii* with *R. ambiguum*, the results of which remain in the garden today, and whilst one seedling does merit a second look, others are *R. ambiguum* gone haywire with muddy coloured flowers. However, they do serve as windbreaks in this 20-acre garden and the smaller-leaved varieties do offer nesting sites for songbirds.

Before submitting a clone for registration, I do like to hear the opinions of others, sometimes of praise and occasionally of criticism, such as that from a lady who, when presented with a rather garish camellia seedling, uttered a long, drawn-out "No".

One day when visiting my trial ground in a rather neglected stretch of woodland, an old friend, Trevor Crosby, eminent horticulturist and active Group member, exclaimed, "Now I do like that one with the red flush". From the cross *R. selense* x *R.* Fabia Group, it was promptly named *R.* 'Holiad Trevor' – Pant-yr-Holiad being the name of my garden in west Wales – and transplanted to a kinder environment in the garden. Now some three metres in height, it is, unfortunately, most difficult to propagate from cuttings, half-ripe wood rarely appearing on current year's growth and grafting or layering the only recourse. Lack of ripening may be due to growing in too much shade and fairly high temperatures during recent autumns. However, a rooted layer growing in a more open situation offers hope for suitable cutting material in the future.

RHODODENDRON 'Holiad Yellow Beauty'   JAMES GOUGH

In memory of such a knowledgeable gardener, who I regarded as my personal vade-mecum, I would like to see this clone more widely distributed.

An obituary to Trevor appeared in the RCMG Bulletin of November 2005. Sadly, that era had also recorded the death of another valued member, Margaret Jennings of Gelli Deg garden in nearby Carmarthenshire, then home also to Trevor, who, in caring for the garden, introduced so many good plants. On visiting the garden a few years ago, I was confronted by a vista of pink blossom, framed by the foliage of later flowering rhododendrons. On closer examination, I discovered that sheet of colour to be R. 'Holiad Michelle', one of my earlier hybrids from crossing R. cinnabarinum with R. carolinianum, registered in 1990.

RHODODENDRON 'Holiad Michelle'   JAMES GOUGH

Largely ignored by past hybridists, the American R. carolinianum offers potential for creating rhododendrons suitable for the restricted gardens of today. With small leaves, generous sprays of flower, hardy in the extreme and compact growth, not attaining two metres in stature after some thirty years, this species does appear to pass these characteristics on to its progeny.

Crossed with R. scabrifolium var. spiciferum, R. carolinianum produced another worthwhile hybrid, flowering somewhat earlier than its half-sibling. Planted in close proximity to R. 'May Day', the plant was reduced to poking through the dense foliage of its companion, but brightening the scene with a few sprays of bright pink flowers in April.

Moving the plant was fraught with difficulties, but cuttings rooted easily and some youngsters are now growing without competition, but this clone does grow in a rather leggy fashion and pinching-out will probably be required to produce a more compact habit.

A cross of R. wardii and R. Elizabeth Group produced another load of rubbish, with one progeny growing into an umbrella-shaped small tree bearing rather plain pink flowers. Not producing the desired colour, its demise was halted by my wife exclaiming, 'I do like that one'. Reluctantly, I registered it as 'Brenda's Choice'. Grown as an isolated specimen, the shape is attractive and probably due to the 'Creeping Jenny' form of R. Elizabeth Group being used in the cross. (Incidentally, I have grown second generation plants from this clone of R. Elizabeth Group, where the prostrate habit has disappeared, flowering is later and foliage different. Continuance of generative culture might well produce the parent R. griersonianum. Is this evidence of Nature abhorring hybridization?)

Of course, plants do cross in the wild, but in the Himalayas flowering times of individual species are largely governed by altitude and do not coincide. Furthermore, many chance hybrids are sterile and I have seen one large-leaved specimen where the stamens were completely devoid of anthers.

However, complications arise with my seedlings of R. 'Planetum', once considered a species, but now thought to be a natural cross of R. fortunei and R. sutchuenense and yet the progeny has replicated its parent. This genus is full of enigmas, which might be the reason for such a dedicated following.

Another use of R. Elizabeth Group was in the production of 'Holiad Brenda', where crossing with R. Carmen Group produced a semi-dwarf with flowers of tessellated bright pink occurring in late June and sometimes into July.

Unfortunately, the plant is not the easiest to cultivate, requiring an open and protected site, but is a welcome show of colour rather late in the season.

The blooming of *R. selense*, a mountain rhododendron from China and once almost lost to cultivation in Britain, prompted me to continue hybridizing.

After much thought, I opted for crossing with *R.* Fabia Group, where *R. griersonianum* might add late flowering and *R. dichroanthum* some variety of colouration.

From a hundred seedlings grown-on to flowering, about a dozen were worthy of consideration and finally, six distinct clones were submitted for registration. The remainder of the reserved batch were not significantly different and were retained as 'Garden Hybrids', while the remaining eighty-odd were discarded as worthless.

Favourites among my own hybrids, seedlings from *R. selense* x *R.* Fabia Group offer a good selection of colour, flower in June with a lax truss and perform at an early age, but the influence of *R. selense* is only too plain, culminating in potential monsters and hardly fit for the smaller gardens of today, but plants are always welcomed by those with larger expanses.

Perhaps my favourite among these is *R.* 'Holiad Strawberry Ripple', the name indicating some similarity with a certain type of ice cream, with red stripes brightening the creamy flowers. By luck, this clone was the first to flower and it was with bated breath that I awaited flowering of the remaining crosses.

Another season and many more were in bloom, with *R.* 'Holiad Yellow Beauty' stealing the show. Pink in bud and opening to deep yellow, presumably gained from *R. dichroanthum* being a grandparent, the plant is a welcome splash of colour in early June, a time when yellow-flowered rhododendrons are scarce.

Not that all sister seedlings are without a touch of this colour with *R.* 'Holiad Glenda Gough' ageing to a rich cream, but always with a touch of pink in the petals.

Named after a lady who helped towards the garden's development in early days, I can remember her weeding freshly turned soil in what are now beds so crammed with plants that interlopers have little chance.

Passed by countless times in the trial woodland, a pink with crimson flushing to the petals was rescued from growing in chaos where our badgers have covered so many rhododendrons with excavated earth. Initially a sorry sight, it was christened *R.* 'Holiad Blush' and is now quite a handsome plant.

Last of these seedlings to be registered, *R.* 'Holiad Caroline Llewellyn' bears nearly white flowers edged and striped with red. Set against the bright green foliage of the progeny of this cross in general, there are the colours of Wales, and in deference to my wife's ancestry and a country where growing the genus is comparatively easy, this one was named after my good lady's forebears and as a personal thank you for tolerating my addiction to rhododendrons for more that half a century. But, however tempted, I have no aspirations to clip the bush into a topiary representation of a Welsh dragon!

RHODODENDRON 'Brenda's Choice'

JAMES GOUGH

RHODODENDRON 'Strawberry Ripple'   JAMES GOUGH

On a more serious note, I am pleased that although Group registration is still permitted, it has largely given way to that of individual clones. No longer will we have the anomaly of an AM clone of a Group being different to that awarded FCC as is the case with the Elizabeth or Inamorata Groups, for example.

Not that the rules are so clear in respect of second generation hybrids, where selfing of the original sometimes produces a superior form. Some years ago, I selfed R. 'Holiad Caroline Llewellyn', the first of which is now flowering and one does show evidence of improved flowers, but I might let sleeping dogs lie and hope the engraved name plate will stand the test of time.

My last and probably final registration was not a hybrid, but a selected seedling of R. aberconwayi. Long ago, I received seed of R. aberconwayi, courtesy of The Commissioners of Crown Lands, Windsor. Among the plants raised was one with a capitate style of truss heavily spotted with red. Flowering profusely, it is always a pillar of blossom in early May and I was being badgered on all sides to register it.

A couple of years ago, a presentation plant was required for Earl Lloyd George in commemoration of his octogenarian status and in recognition of the great work he had undertaken in restoring a large Welsh historic garden at Ffynone.

But first, I had to confirm that this rhododendron was R. aberconwayi and not a hybrid. Descriptions, foliage and photographs were despatched to the Registrar and very encouraging words received in reply. Today, R. aberconwayi 'Earl Lloyd George' is growing in several gardens and should survive beyond my time.

RHODODENDRON 'Glenda Gough'   JAMES GOUGH

Avoiding the attraction of crossing elepidote with lepidote, which is rarely successful and may result in progeny of weak constitution with limited life expectancy, the azaleodendrons deserve a new appraisal.

In this context, it would be interesting to repeat some crosses of yesteryear with *R.* Hybridum Group (*maximum* x *viscosum*) raised in 1817 and *R.* Cartonii Group (*catawbiense* x *nudiflorum*) raised in 1825 being among the first to appear in cultivation. Then, we might enjoy the flowers of our forefathers, before the introduction of more exotic species.

On the practical side, a good quality camelhair brush remains the best for imitating the work of a bee and I find that early morning is the best time for pollinating. Once the sun desiccates a stigma, it will not accept pollen.

Weatherproof labelling of pollinated flowers is important, for six months may elapse before gathering seed. Both before and after pollination, provision against insects is necessary and paper bags are superior to plastic.

For registration, one must comply with more than 32 articles as published in the International Code of Nomenclature for Cultivated Plants. State the reason for the choice of name – outlandish made-up names are no longer in fashion (but are not forbidden!) Reference to the RHS Colour Chart is preferred, as is sound botanical knowledge and good

RHODODENDRON ABERCONWAYI
'Earl Lloyd George'

JAMES GOUGH

photographs are appreciated. The Registrar has proved most helpful in all respects.

Above all, do spread your hybrids around. Into trade if possible, show them, give plants to friends, relations and anyone else who will appreciate your efforts. Only then will they stand the test of time and not become merely names in the International Register!

Geoff Taylor

is a longstanding member of the Group and former Bulletin Editor

Finding Mr Wilson

MARK FLANAGAN

FOR AFICIONADOS OF THE GREAT Edwardian plant hunter Ernest Henry Wilson, 2008 represents an important centenary. For his third visit to China, between 1907 and 1909, Wilson was contracted by the Arnold Arboretum. Charles Sprague Sargent, the patrician director of the Arnold, recognised Wilson as the supreme botanical collector and worked tirelessly to engage him. At the age of 31, Wilson was at the height of his powers, his two previous trips to the East had taught him how best to organise his travel, how to maintain a harmonious existence with the native peoples of China and had given him an in-depth under-standing of the flora and geography of western and central China. As Wilson left for China in late December 1906, this third visit was to prove his most successful and 1908, in particular, his most adventurous and productive year.

What is seldom recognised are the enormous distances that Wilson covered – much more ground than his contemporaries. As soon as the season began in spring, Wilson was on the move and he didn't stop until the autumn seed harvest was secured some 9 or 10 months later. During the summer of 1908 Wilson undertook two stupendous journeys covering over 1500 kilometres of the roughest terrain. As a frequent visitor to Sichuan I have often caught hints of Wilson's comings and goings but, to my knowledge, few if any people have sought to pin down his exact routes. A further incentive to undertaking such a task was to compare how the country had changed in the intervening century, given the great convulsions that China has undergone. When Wilson travelled in China he was in a land that had been governed by emperors for over two millennia.

During his travels for the Arnold Arboretum, Wilson kept a wonderful photographic record of the plants, landscapes and people of Imperial China and this also provided a challenge to try and re-trace his journeys and to match his images to the present day situation. Unfortunately, though an extensive author, none of Wilson's writings are presented as a contiguous travelogue, in the manner of Frank Kingdon-Ward. His most famous book *China, Mother of Gardens* is more a series of vignettes of his travels accompanied by essays of the products, customs and natural resources of China. It is necessary, therefore, to consult a wide range of sources to construct an itinerary of Wilson's travels.

In the summer of 2005 I put together a set of plans to try and track Wilson's routes in China. In this I had an enthusiastic ally in my long-time field confederate Tony Kirkham, the Head of the Arboretum at Kew, another Wilson devotee. Tony and I visited the Arnold Arboretum in October of that year to consult the Wilson archive. By reference to Wilson's field journals and correspondence and with the help of Librarian Lisa Pearson and Director of Living Collections Peter del Tredici we were able to fill in virtually all the gaps in our knowledge of Wilson's journeys that had been garnered from his published works. I was confident that, with support on the ground in China, we would be able to retrace significant sections of Wilson's travels and add to our rather scanty knowledge of his field activities.

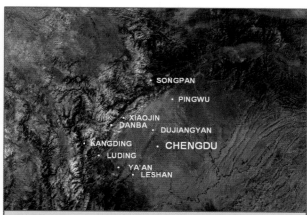

WESTERN AND NORTHERN SICHUAN showing the route taken by Mark Flanagan and Tony Kirkham

SATELLITE IMAGE © DORLING KINDERSLEY

Having been part of the Kew-led SICH consortium of collectors (SICH being a collector's code – a shortened version of Sichuan), I knew exactly who to go to for in-country help – Yin Kaipu and Zhong Shengxian of the Institute of Biology in Chengdu coordinated all the trips and Dr Yin, in particular, proved to have an unrivalled knowledge of Sichuan. We had discussed, in outline, our ideas on a previous collecting trip and so when we approached them with a more fully determined scheme we found a ready audience. We quickly agreed that June 2006 would be the due date and that a trip which described two circular routes in the west and north-central part of the province would allow us to follow important sections of Wilson's journeys of 1903, and particularly 1908 and 1910 (see map). What had taken Wilson many weeks to complete we would try and accomplish in just 16 days! Though this

sounds faintly ridiculous, the vastly improved roads in modern China and the use of a 4-wheel drive vehicle gave us more than a fighting chance.

Things began well at Leshan (Kiating to Wilson and an important winter base), where we were able to locate the position where Wilson took his photograph of the city walls and where he stood to take his image of the confluence of the Min and Dadu rivers close to the famous rock-carved giant Buddha. Next it was an ascent of Wa-wu Shan, greatly facilitated by a cable-car which now ascends close to the summit. The mountain is exactly as Wilson describes it:

'…an extraordinary-looking massive mountain,…resembling a huge ark floating above the clouds.'

It is one of the three sacred mountains of Sichuan along with the better known Emei Shan and Wa Shan and, like its sister peaks, it rises from the edge of the Chengdu Plain a great lump of hard rock which resisted the erosive forces that swept away the rest of the surrounding plain. Due to the verticality of the slopes, the cable car ride is an exhilarating one and it is clear that a good deal of regeneration has taken place on the mountain sides since Wilson's time who comments unfavourably about the lack of both diversity and maturity on the mountain. Mixed in with the general woody vegetation we saw big specimens of *Rhododendron calophytum* var. *openshawianum*, just past flowering; closer to the woodland floor could be seen *R. wiltonii* with characteristic deeply rugose leaves. The summit is flat, *'…undulating, park-like and covered with an impenetrable jungle of bamboo-scrub about 6 feet high…'*.

From Wa-wu Shan we journeyed north, spending the night in Ya'an before turning west into the valley of the Dadu River via the tunnel through Erlang Shan. This placed us firmly back in Wilson territory as he traversed this river valley (known to him as the Tung River) on many occasions. At the small town of Lengji occurs a very large ginkgo, purported to be

1,700 years old. Wilson visited Lengji and took several photographs but unfortunately recent construction around the tree makes it impossible to occupy the position where he took his images and renders it difficult to capture the scale and impressiveness of this immense tree. It still appears in reasonable health, though full of dead wood.

On to Moxi where a famous image of Wilson's, an ancient Chinese fir (*Cunninghamia lanceolata*) was taken. Sadly this tree was destroyed in a fire in the early 1990s and though the temple at its foot was rebuilt, the tree remains a sad, scorched shell. We lit an incense stick for Wilson at the foot of the tree where a small sapling has been planted to try and recapture the glory of the original tree – it has a long, long way to go.

At Kangding we were on familiar ground. Tony and I have travelled to this unique place on three occasions and Wilson was a frequent visitor. As well as being a great trading town it is also the gateway to the high mountains where Sichuan meets Tibet – the Da Xue Shan (Big Snow Mountains). A particular highlight was the drive to the Ya-jia pass, beautiful flowering shrubs of *Rhododendron souliei* being common on the ascent. This pass is much less well-known than the more frequently visited Zheduo pass, to the north, which carries the main road to distant Lhasa. It was below the Ya-jia pass that Wilson collected the lampshade poppy (*Meconopsis integrifolia*), the principal object of his second expedition, on 16 July 1903. We were not disappointed, as the poppy occurs in countless thousands along with a whole host of other gems including *Primula secundiflora*, *Cypripedium tibeticum* and *Rheum alexandre*. Great masses of *Rhododendron przewalskii* were another highlight, but we noted with interest that many of the flowers had been damaged by frost – not just a problem in English gardens! Wilson tells us of the fearsome reputation that the Ya-jia pass had amongst his Chinese, who were not by nature or inclination, mountain people – '*This...pass enjoys an unenviable reputation, and is much dreaded on account of its asphyxiating winds. It is said to be the only pass in the neighbourhood which "stops people's breath".*' On reaching the pass we were forced to concur, for although it was June 17, the temperature hovered around freezing point and a biting wind blew from the west bringing pulses of sleet in its wake. Despite this, we were thrilled to take an image from almost exactly the same spot as Wilson when he re-visited the pass on 19 July 1908.

The Da Xue Shan and the neighbouring ranges are part of the vast, complex Hengduan Shan which form the eastern extension of the Himalayas, created at the same time but, due to the shearing effect involved when the landmass of India collided with the Asian continent, they incline north/south. The mountains, eroded by melt-water and monsoon-swollen rivers – the Jinshsa, Yalong, Dadu and Min – form an enormous convoluted mass of peaks, ridges and spurs with deep, sheer-sided valleys. The range climaxes at the summit of the mighty Gongga Shan which, at 7556 metres is Sichuan's highest mountain by some way. Gongga

RHEUM ALEXANDRE, an attractive and striking herb in the flower-rich meadows below the Ya-jia pass.

TONY KIRKHAM

RHODODENDRON PRZEWALSKII covers large areas on the high mountains of the Da Xue Shan. At the Ya-jia pass it can be found at nearly 4000m.

TONY KIRKHAM

Shan was brought to the attention of the West by Joseph Rock in 1930 (under its Tibetan name of Minya Konka) when he infamously over-estimated its height, erroneously claiming it to be higher than Mount Everest. This mountain has always intrigued me, though dominating the area it is frequently covered in cloud and on five separate occasions I have journeyed to key vantage points and been disappointed to find a shroud-covered summit. Another intriguing aspect is that in all his writings Wilson never mentions it. How can this be? He spent many months in the Da Xue Shan, surely he must have heard some local reference to the peak or glimpsed some distant view. The obvious conclusion was that he too was unlucky.

As Tony and I wandered the lonely slopes around the Ya-jia pass I pondered this matter, knowing that the giant mountain lay to the southwest of our position. All around us were shattered and snow-clad peaks and it would need a strenuous hike into the higher reaches to breast these in order to provide an unencumbered view to the southwest and time didn't allow this opportunity. In the warmth and comfort of our 4x4 as we took the road

back to Kangding, I re-read Wilson's account of his first journey to the Ya-jia pass which was published in the Gardeners' Chronicle as *Leaves from my Chinese Note-book* in 1906. One paragraph leapt from the page, and although I had pored over all Wilson's writings for the best part of 18 months the significance of the words had previously escaped me. '*The moraine in front of us terminated in tremendous fields of ice, glaciers of a virgin peak 21,000 feet high. The sun shone brilliantly and we got a magnificent view of the surrounding mountains. South, south-west of us lay a gigantic peak, several thousand feet higher than the one mentioned; its summit crowned with snowfields of enormous size.*' Gongga Shan? Surely.

Pressing on, our road carried us to the north, in fact the reverse of Wilson's arduous 1908 journey between Chengdu and Kangding. The Da Xue Shan give way to another range called the Da Pao Shan (Big Cannon Mountains). Wilson travelled south and on the eastern side of this range but we had to take the western side through the extensive grasslands that lead into Tibet. The turf was studded with gorgeous plants – *Incarvillea delavayi, Meconopsis horridula, Lilium lophophorum* – odd plants of *Rhododendron*

THE YA-JIA PASS was visited by Wilson twice and on his second visit in 1908 he took this image, the scene remains unchanged today

ABOVE: E H WILSON © ARNOLD ARBORETUM AND BELOW: TONY KIRKHAM

capitatum formed hummocky mounds amongst the grass sward and the horizon was an endless, undulating green line. We rejoined Wilson's route north of the Da Pao Shan where a slow-moving river emerged and the forest returned, a wonderful assemblage of stately conifers (including the striking flaky fir *Abies squamata*) and diverse broadleaved trees – *'a magnificent fragment of virgin forest'*. The road skirted the river and led into a tight, vertically sided valley – *'a narrow, savage, magnificently wooded ravine'*. All along the river valley were small villages mentioned by Wilson – Tung-ku, T'ung-lu-fang and Mao-niu – the road had a level, macadam surface allowing for rapid transport, very different from Wilson's day – *'My head coolie declared it was the worst road we had ever traversed, and I was inclined to agree with him'*. We stopped at Mao-niu (Yak village) to check directions. The village is exactly as described by Wilson – *'a fair sized village for the country... mainly perched on a flat 200 feet above the torrent...'*. Intriguingly, we were told of a village story, passed down through several generations, which relates the visit of a foreigner interested in plants.

This Mao-niu river emerged from its valley at Danba (Romi Chango to Wilson) where it is joined by the Dadu river and a little further along by the Xiao Chin He (Little Gold River). The combined waters take the name and southerly course of the Dadu eventually joining the Min at Leshan. Danba and the surrounding area are of more than ordinary interest. The historical boundary between China and Tibet was never well defined but many travellers, including Wilson, recognised that it lay, de facto, along the territory between Songpan and Kangding. This conclusion was partly based on anthropological evidence as the area is peopled by diverse groups, most of which are Tibetan in origin. Wilson writes extensively and with evident interest about the many different peoples he encountered – their appearance, manners and customs. A feature of the countryside near Danba is the presence of various striking stone and brick towers, many up to 30 metres in height, whose purpose seems to have been mainly defensive. In the 18th century the Chinese, under the impetus of their ambitious Manchu emperors, were pushing west, conquering and subjugating all the local tribes in order to secure their borders. The valleys towards Danba witnessed ferocious fighting with great loss of life on both sides before the Chinese were finally triumphant. Today all the ethnic minorities in China, and there are 55, mainly in the west, enjoy a degree of freedom of expression and a respect for their traditions.

The road turned to the east along the Little Gold River and we passed through Xiaojin (Monkong Ting to Wilson) before beginning the climb to the Balang Shan pass, which lies on the watershed separating the Dadu and Min rivers. We were treated to a wonderful view of the Siguniang Shan (Four Girls Mountain), as the name suggests a series of four peaks the highest of which, at 6250 metres, is Sichuan's second

The turf was studded with gorgeous plants ... the horizon was an endless undulating green line.

highest mountain. Once again Wilson is mute on this subject and one can only assume they were cloud covered when he passed the same point on 25 June 1908. Leaving the woodlands behind, the road snaked up towards the pass, rhododendron heathland dominates, principally composed of *R. nivale* ssp *boreale,* interspersed with the red poppywort (*Meconopsis punicea*) and the exquisite *Primula melanops*. Inevitably, the conditions deteriorated and we crossed the pass through a low dense cloud not dissimilar to the conditions endured by Wilson *'...we toiled slowly over the dreaded Pan-lan Shan, crossing the pass in a dense, driving, bitterly cold mist.'*

The east side of the pass fell quickly away and we sped on towards Dujiangyan but not before a highlight that I had particularly waited for. Wilson talks rapturously about the flora of the alpine meadows below the Balang Shan. *'All the moorland areas are covered so thickly with the Tibetan lady-slipper orchid (Cypripedium tibeticum) that it was impossible to step without treading on the huge dark red flowers ...Yet the most fascinating herb of all was the extraordinary* Primula *(now*

THE STUNNING PANORAMA of the Four Girls Mountain, a scene not witnessed by E H Wilson despite passing this very point.

TONY KIRKHAM

nature's wonders. As the trees returned, straggly bushes of *Rhododendron balangense* and *R. galactinum* could be seen at the forest edges.

At Dujiangyan we prepared for the next part of our breakneck journey. In 1910 Wilson undertook a trip north to Songpan. Having previously visited this town by two well-used roads he took a little-known route which lay between. This journey is perhaps best known for its return leg, for it was in the lower Min valley on September 4 1910 that he met with the accident that was to end his plant hunting career in China.

The first part of the journey was through heavily cultivated country and was of interest only in locating several of the charac-

Omphalogramma) vincaeflora …*This most un-primrose-like primula is very abundant in grassy places.*' Once again the literal truth of Wilson's writing was revealed; the orchids and associated plants are so abundant as to be impossible not to step on. The display is one of

terful bridges that Wilson photographed. As the hills began to close in we reluctantly had to depart from Wilson's route which becomes a foot-traffic only path beyond the village of Xiao Ba. A circuitous detour took us to Yeh-tang where we 'rejoined' Wilson. On 19 August 1910

RHODODENDRON GALACTINUM raised from Wilson's original collection (W4254) below the Balang Shan pass, flowering in the Rhododendron Species Collection in the Valley Gardens, Windsor Great Park.

MARK FLANAGAN

IN JUNE the Balang Shan is a natural flower garden dominated by exquisite plants such as the slipper orchid, *Cypripedium tibeticum*, and the primula relative *Omphalogramma vincaeflorum*.

TONY KIRKHAM

Wilson photographed a huge old tree of the rare and unusual *Meliosma beaniana* here. We were told that the tree was still alive and with a great sense of anticipation we arrived at the village. Sure enough the old tree still dominates the village and is a remarkable link back to Wilson's time. He much admired this species and the closely related *M. veitchiorum*. To my knowledge *M. beaniana* is represented by just two trees in cultivation, both from Wilson's seed, one at the Royal Botanic Garden, Edinburgh the other at Caerhays.

Back on the road, we were now able to follow Wilson's route directly. The old garrison town of Xiao He is just as described and photographed by Wilson, with the remains of the old monastery still visible. The recently surfaced road continued all the way to Huanglong, leaving the Fu river valley by a series of 12 hairpin bends; Wilson's exit from the valley was by an exhausting scramble up the hillside. Specimens of *Magnolia dawsoniana* populated the slopes and must present a stunning spectacle in the early spring. The village of San Tsze where Wilson had a *'violent fit of ague'* seemed little changed in the interval. A 95-year-old man

claimed his father met a westerner answering to Wilson's description!

We passed into the Huanglong Scenic and Historic Area, now a World Heritage Site. This amazing place captivates all who are fortunate enough to encounter it. Wilson, in his understated way, calls it *'a most interesting place'*. The central area of the site – Huanglongguo (Yellow Dragon Valley) – falls steeply from the snow-clad heights of Xue Bao Ding (Snow Mountain Peak), at 5558 metres the highest point in the Min Shan, over a relatively short distance creating a corrugated slope down which the melting snow brings water charged with lime which precipitates out of solution to form pools and tarns each holding azure coloured water, with the giant mountain in the background a magical scene is created. On the floor, the Tibetan ladies' slipper orchid was frequent as was its yellow-flowered counterpart – *Cypripedium flavum*. In the shade of the forest *Rhododendron watsonii* was common as were *R. rufum* and *R. oreodoxa*.

Songpan was Wilson's favourite town in Sichuan and it continues to hold a fascination for western visitors. It is an entry to some very

THE STRIKING VILLAGE of Pai Shan Yin sits atop a hillock in the Min River Valley. Wilson stayed here on the night of 30th August 1910, just 4 days before his near-fatal accident.

ABOVE: E H WILSON © ARNOLD ARBORETUM AND BELOW: TONY KIRKHAM

number of small sections of wall were evident, but little else. In revisiting I was delighted to see that the whole circumference had been re-built and in a most impressive way, the town has been returned to much as Wilson would have known it. We climbed the surrounding hills and attempted to match the images Wilson took of the town in 1910, with a fair degree of success.

Leaving Songpan the following day we drove south down the valley of the Min River. Wilson left Songpan on the same road on 27 August 1910 little realising that he would meet with a near fatal accident just 8 days later. The final part of our trip was to try and find the place where Wilson's accident occurred. Once again we passed the landmarks and villages that Wilson mentions, including the attractive village of Pai Shan Yin known to Wilson as Shih Ta Kuan ' *…perhaps the most prettily situated village of the whole route.'* This was followed by Yanmen and finally Sian Son Qiao, the last place Wilson stayed before his accident. There was little to go on as to the exact spot where Wilson was caught in the landslip which broke his right leg in two places, necessitating a life-saving dash to Chengdu and the ministrations of Dr Davidson at the Friends' Mission. We conjectured that a morning's journey would have taken him perhaps 7–8 kilometres and after this distance we pulled up to reconnoitre. Interestingly, a new road has been built on the western bank of the river as the old road on the eastern bank was closed due to the treacherous

interesting country, either north into the neighbouring province of Gansu or west into the high mountains. Wilson knew Songpan as a walled garrison town on the edge of very lawless country. During the Japanese invasion of China, prior to and during the Second World War, Songpan was bombed and lost much of its protective wall. When I first visited here in 2003 the great north gate was extant and a

XUE BAO DING, the highest peak in the Min Shan range, dominates the stunning Huanglong valley. The mountain contains the most easterly glacier in China

MARK FLANAGAN

nature of the hillsides which flank it and the frequency of dangerous rock falls which occurred. The place we stopped at was named Fu Tang Ba and this seemed as likely as anywhere to have been the place where the great plant hunter met his fate. Poignantly, on the hillsides above were masses of the regal lily, one of Wilson's finest introductions and the reason why he was journeying down the Min River in the first place.

Just prior to his final departure from China, Wilson wrote to Sargent. *'I have enjoyed my work in China and am proud in the knowledge that I have been privileged to achieve success in worthy employ and am certainly not going to pull a long face because the Fates have unkindly given me a parting kick.'*

At the end of this trip both Tony and I felt privileged to have followed in the wake of the great man and to have unravelled some of the hitherto unknown aspects of his many travels.

ACKNOWLEDGMENTS

With grateful thanks to the Arnold Arboretum for granting permission to reproduce the original images by and of Ernest Henry Wilson.

Mark Flanagan

is Keeper of the Gardens at Windsor Great Park

Wilson study day 2007

MIKE ROBINSON

PROMPTED BY THE JOURNEYS of Mark Flanagan and Tony Kirkham described in the previous article, and by their renewed interest in assembling a collection of his plants, the Group organised a study day on 'Chinese' Wilson on April 4th 2007, when around a hundred people assembled in London to be treated to a review of Wilson's life and achievements and an attempt to set his contributions to horticulture into context.

It was a revelation to almost all present that much of the landscape and vegetation through which Wilson travelled in Sichuan is still present today, and a pleasing relief to see from Mark and Tony's photographs that in this province of China at least, the environment is still in good shape with many of Wilson's plants still thriving, with little sign of the deforestation we all dread. Their painstaking and scientific quest is an encouraging antidote to the speculation by others with little first-hand knowledge.

Following a most interesting illustrated biography of the great man from Roy Briggs, who described, with many contemporary illustrations, Wilson's family, career, his hardships relating to travel and the demanding nature of his sponsors, much of the day was spent looking at the plants he discovered and introduced.

Members of the Group will, of course, realise the importance of the discoveries and introductions within our three genera – almost every rhododendron collection will include species Wilson introduced or the many hybrids derived from them. One has only to mention *Rhododendron calophytum*, *R. sutchuenense*, *R. davidsonianum*, *R. lutescens* and *R. moupinense* to get the picture, and this without mentioning the 'Wilson 50' Kurume azaleas which have had such a seminal effect.

Jim Gardiner described Wilson's magnolia introductions, which have perhaps had an even more far reaching effect than the rhododendrons, although fewer species were brought back from the wild: *Magnolia wilsonii* naturally, *M. dawsoniana*, *M. sargentiana* var. *robusta* and *M. sprengeri* var. *diva*. It is hard to imagine a collection of magnolias without these or their progeny. Jim's superb slides of the hybrids derived from these species, especially *M. sprengeri*, revealed the remarkable richness and variety Wilson contributed to gardens all over the world..

However, what the study day brought into sharp focus was that the total number of introductions by Wilson was simply staggering, and many more than those of almost every other plant collector, earlier or later. Many of these plants form the backbone of gardens and arboreta all over the world.

In his first expedition to Western Hubei and Sichuan for the Veitch nursery, Wilson introduced many of the species previously described from herbaria sent to Paris by French missionaries, but his later foray for Veitch and those for the Arnold Arboretum resulted in the discovery of hundreds of new species as well as their introduction.

Maurice Foster reminded us that Wilson's original quest was famously related to the introduction of *Davidia involucrata*, but then he had the unenviable task of selecting the most significant woody plants from the thousand or so described in the three volumes of *Plantae Wilsonianae*: *Acer griseum* and *A. davidii*, *Albizia julibrissin*, many berberis including *Berberis wilsoniae*, *Betula albosinensis*, *Camellia cuspidata*, *Cornus kousa* var. *chinensis*, *Kolkwitzia amabilis*, *Prunus serrula* and *P. conradinae*, *Rosa moyesii* and *R. filipes*, many sorbus including *Sorbus hupehensis* and viburnums including *Viburnum betulifolium*.

Among the noteworthy climbers brought back were *Actinidia deliciosa* (the kiwi fruit – formerly known as *A. chinensis*), *Clematis armandii*, and *Lonicera tragophylla*.

Wilson's second quest for Veitch was to introduce the beautiful *Meconopsis integrifolia*. Chris Grey-Wilson gave us a lightning tour of the non-woody plants of note: *Abelia schumannii*, *Aconitum carmichaelii* var. *wilsonii*,

Astilbe grandis, Corydalis wilsonii, Cypripedium flavum and *C. tibeticum, Iris wilsonii, Ligularia dentata, Meconopsis punicea,* many primulas including *Primula pulverulenta* and *P. polyneura* and *Thalictrum delavayi.* Naturally Chris concluded with the regal lily, *Lilium regale,* perhaps the species which Wilson was most pleased to have introduced.

With such a wealth and diversity of plants it would be a thrill to find a garden in which they are grown together in a similar admixture to that found in the wild – woody plants in wide variety with climbers twining through them and a planting of bulbs and herbaceous growing around and through. It would, as well, be a scholarly garden, as the planner would have to research with considerable care the plant associations found by the great man: but what a challenge for the 21st century, and a fitting memorial to Ernest 'Chinese' Wilson.

Bibliography ■ Briggs Roy W. (1993), *'Chinese' Wilson,* (HMSO). C. S. Sargent 1916 (ed.), *Plantae Wilsonianae,* (Dioscorides Press, 3 volumes, 1998)

Further reference ■ www.nccpg.com/Gloucestershire/wilson1.html

Evaluation of cold hardiness and ornamental characteristics of Korean provenances of *Camellia japonica*

ANTHONY S AIELLO, ELINOR I GOFF, SHELLEY DILLARD & MICHELLE CONNERS

FOR THE PAST QUARTER-CENTURY one of the primary missions of the Morris Arboretum of the University of Pennsylvania has been domestic and international plant exploration and evaluation. Since the late 1970s, staff of the Arboretum have participated in 19 plant collecting trips, including expeditions to South Korea, China, the Caucasus Mountains and within the United States. Seed is collected primarily and returned to the Arboretum for propagation and these trips have resulted in a living collection that contains approximately 4,000 plants of wild-collected and documented origin, representing just over 900 taxa. Our collection has broad holdings in woody plants suitable for the mid-Atlantic region of the United States with particular strengths in conifers, *Hamamelis, Acer, Magnolia, Ilex* and *Quercus*.

The goals of the Arboretum's plant exploration and evaluation program are to:
• Broaden the genetic pool of known species, including:
 – Broadening adaptability to difficult microclimates
 – Extending hardiness and increasing vigor
• Increase insect and disease resistance
• Conserve rare and endangered species
• Select improved horticultural forms
• Evaluate and introduce appropriate new species

Between 1979 and 1991, Arboretum staff participated in five collecting expeditions to South Korea planned to sequentially cover different geographic regions within the country. The 1984 Expedition to Korea Northwestern Coast and Islands (Korea Northwest Expedition – KNW) visited areas along the northwestern coast and inland to the Kwangnung Arboretum (now Korea National Arboretum) of South Korea (Meyer 1985, Yinger 1989). It is from this 1984 expedition that the Arboretum holds a number of accessions of *Camellia japonica* collected on Taechong and Sochong Islands, off the northwest coast of South Korea. The island collections represent some of the most northern collections ever made of common camellia.

From the late 1970s into the early 1980s a series of extremely cold winters devastated camellia collections at the US National Arboretum and

CAMELLIA JAPONICA plants growing in a garden setting at the Morris Arboretum

ANTHONY AIELLO

elsewhere in the Washington, DC area (Ackerman and Egolf 1991; Ackerman and Egolf 1992). These severe winters, and the damage to large numbers of cultivars, inspired Dr. William Ackerman of the US National Arboretum and others to undertake breeding programs to develop truly cold-hardy camellias (USDA zones 6 and 7). In light of this research, the northern collections of *Camellia japonica* from South Korea were thought to have potential to expand the hardiness of common camellia, generally considered to be reliably hardy in USDA hardiness zone 7b (Flint 1997) but historically not reliably cold hardy in the Philadelphia area (Zone 6b; average annual minimum temperatures between –23°C and –18°C).

Evidence from freezing tests supported the hypothesis that the Korean accessions of *Camellia japonica* possessed greater cold hardiness than other selections of this species. Dirr *et al.* (1993) reported that one of the Korean accessions of *Camellia japonica* (MOAR # 86-050/KNW 352) had stems that were cold hardy from –24°C to –30°C, indicating that these collections held promise for extending the potentially useful range of this species.

Given the northern locations of the Korean *Camellia japonica* populations and in conjunction with the freezing test evidence, the Arboretum undertook a long-term field and garden trial of several accessions. Since the late 1980s plants grown from these collections have been evaluated for cold hardiness and several ornamental characteristics. The camellias in this study all exhibit attractive evergreen foliage and single red flowers. These plants are large shrubs, reaching up to 12 feet tall in 20 years. This article reports on twenty

AREAS VISITED on the 1984 Korea Northwest collecting expedition

years of evaluation of *Camellia japonica* with known provenances collected on the 1984 expedition to northwest South Korea.

PROCEDURE AND RESULTS OF EVALUATIONS

In 1984, nine seed accessions of *Camellia japonica* were collected on two islands off the coast of northwest South Korea: Taechong Do and Sochong Do (Meyer 1985, Yinger 1989). Seeds were sown at the Morris Arboretum beginning in November 1984. Eight of the nine accessions germinated successfully, with varying numbers of seedlings among accessions (Table 1). Plants were accessioned in 1986 and designated for one of two parallel evaluation studies: either a replicated field trial or garden settings throughout the Arboretum. Of the eight successfully germinated accessions, six were eventually planted in the Arboretum's research area or throughout the Arboretum (Tables 2 & 3).

COLLECTION LOCATION of *Camellia japonica* on Sochong Island, South Korea, 1984   PAUL MEYER

FIELD TRIALS AND INITIAL GARDEN TRIALS

In April 1987, 730 seedlings were planted in a replicated field trial at the Arboretum's Bloomfield Farm research area and were evaluated for cold hardiness (Table 2). These 730 plants were planted in a randomized block design with varying light levels. Equal numbers of each accession were divided among the plots and randomly assigned to a location within a plot. From 1989 to 1993 all of these plants were evaluated for general foliage quality, vigor and hardiness (survival) on a scale of 1–5. Ratings were described as follows:

1 – dead
2 – barely surviving
3 – growth slightly stunted
4 – occasional foliar damage
5 – excellent growth and foliar quality

By June 1990, of the 589 surviving plants, 283 had a rating ≥ 3 (growth slightly stunted (Table 2)). Three years later in August 1993, 40 of 170 remaining plants were rated as ≥ 4 (occasional foliar damage (Table 2)). The winters of 1993–94 and 1994–95 resulted in further loss of plants. Between the fall of 1995 and spring of 1999, 25 of these highest rated plants from the original Bloomfield trial were planted into the Arboretum's public garden for further assessment.

In a parallel study, between 1987 and 1991, an additional 33 of the originally germinated seedlings not part of the formal field trial were planted in protected garden settings throughout the Arboretum (Table 3). By October 1999, 22 of these plants remained in the garden (Table 3).

EVALUATION IN GARDEN SETTINGS: 1999–2004

In October 1999, shortly after I arrived at the Morris Arboretum, a total of 50 camellias were alive in garden settings throughout the Arboretum site (Table 3). These included 25 plants from the field trials (Table 2), 22 remaining plants from those originally planted in garden settings (Table 3), and three additional plants which had been cutting-grown in our greenhouse from original seedlings.

Starting in the fall of 1999 and continuing through the spring of 2004 the 50 plants throughout the Arboretum were visually evaluated. In the spring and fall of each year the plants were rated for a variety of ornamental traits including general vigor, hardiness and foliar and floral characteristics.

After these visual evaluations were completed in late 2004, 43 plants remained alive (from the original 763) and each year's ratings for these plants were combined. These 43 plants were divided into three categories according to overall performance and appearance after 5 years of evaluation (Table 3). The top 15 plants ('A' rating) exhibited a consistent positive performance in three key areas of evaluation criteria. The majority of these plants flowered every year, maintained a desirable form and retained glossy foliage throughout the seasons. The middle 16 plants ('B' rating) generally performed well in one or two areas of the evaluation but performance was either not consistent or was poor in the other categories. The lowest rated 12 plants ('C' rating) generally performed poorly in all categories. In some instances, they may have exhibited one positive characteristic but this was overridden by the overall appearance of the plant.

SUMMARY

During 20 years of evaluation of our South Korean accessions of *Camellia japonica*, the vast majority of the original seedlings were culled predominantly based on winter survival or severe

CLOSE-UP of *Camellia japonica* foliage and flower

ANTHONY AIELLO

TABLE 1	*Camellia japonica* seed collected in Taechong and Sochong Islands, South Korea, October 1984. Accessions with germination (+) or no germination(–). Total number of plants planted in field trials at Bloomfield Farm (1987) or in garden settings throughout the Arboretum (1987–91).			
COLLECTION NO.	MOAR ASCENSION NO.	GERMINATION		TOTAL PLANTED
Taechong Island KNW 311	86-292	–		0
KNW 312	86-223	+		28
KNW 342	86-043	+		45
KNW 343	86-044	+		2
KNW 344	86-045	+		100
KNW 345	86-224	+		0*
Sochong Island KNW 348	86-048	+		114
KNW 350	86-049	+		19
KNW 352	86-050	+		455
TOTAL =				763

* One seedling germinated but did not survive.

TABLE 2	Summary of survival and ratings of *Camellia japonica* accessions planted in The Morris Arboretum's field trials at Bloomfield Farm, from 1987 through 1993. Plants evaluated with a rating ≥ 3 showed slightly stunted growth. Plants evaluated with a rating ≥ 4 showed occasional foliar damage.				
COLLECTION NO. MOAR ASCENSION NO.	NO. PLANTED IN TRIALS, APRIL 1987	NO. RATED ≥ 3 JUNE 1990	NO. ALIVE AUGUST 1993	NO. RATED ≥ 4 AUGUST 1993	NO. MOVED FROM FIELD TRIALS TO GARDEN SETTINGS, 1995–99
Taechong Island KNW 312 / 86-223	23	7	3	1	1
KNW 342 / 86-043	35	15	7	4	1
KNW 343 / 86-044	0	–	–	–	–
KNW 344 / 86-045	95	46	25	3	2
KNW 345 / 86-224	0	–	–	–	–
Sochong Island KNW 348 / 86-048	114	39	18	2	3
KNW 350 / 86-049	17	8	5	1	1
KNW 352 / 86-050	446	168	112	29	14
Unknown Plants*					3
TOTAL	730	283	170	40	25*

* Three additional plants whose labels were lost were eventually planted in the Arboretum, to make a total of 25 plants moved from the field trials to garden settings

| TABLE 3 | Summary of *Camellia japonica* accessions planted in garden settings throughout The Morris Arboretum between 1987 through 1991 and supplemented by plantings from 1995 through 2006. | | | | | | | |

COLLECTION NO. MOAR ASCENSION NO.	NO. ORIGINALLY PLANTED IN 1987–91	NO. OF ORIGINAL PLANTS ALIVE AUGUST 1999	NO. MOVED FROM FIELD TRIALS TO GARDEN SETTINGS, 1995-99	ADDITIONAL PLANTS ADDED TO GARDEN SETTINGS, 1999**	TOTAL NO. ALIVE NOVEMBER 2004, WITH RATINGS‡ A B C TOTAL			TOTAL NO. ALIVE JANUARY 2007
Taechong Island KNW 312 / 86-223	5	1	1	–	– 1 1 = 2			2
KNW 342 / 86-043	10	9	1	1	3 1 5 = 9			11
KNW 343 / 86-044	2	0	–	–	–			–
KNW 344 / 86-045	5	3	2	–	2 3 – = 5			5
KNW 345 / 86-224	0	–	–	–	–			–
Sochong Island KNW 348 / 86-048	0	–	3		2 – 1 = 3			2
KNW 350 / 86-049	2	2	1	1	1 2 – = 3			3
KNW 352 / 86-050	9	7	14	–	5 9 4 = 18			18
Unknown Plants*			3	1	2 – 1 = 3			3
TOTAL	33	22*	25*	3*	15 16 12 = 43			44

* As of October 1999, 50 plants total were planted in garden settings throughout the Arboretum.
**Plants cutting-propagated from original seedlings.
‡ These 43 plants were divided into three categories according to overall performance and appearance after 5 years of evaluation.

winter injury. Subsequently, the 50 remaining cold-hardy individuals growing in garden settings were evaluated for a range of horticultural characteristics. These 50, reduced to 43 by 2004 (Table 3), showed sufficient cold hardiness to survive Philadelphia winters from the late 1990s through the present time. As of January 2007, with two additions and one loss, 44 plants are planted throughout the Arboretum (Table 3), representing six of the original nine collections from Korea (KNW 312, 342, 344, 348, 350 & 352). These plants are a valuable genetic resource for introduction and breeding. Although their ornamental value may not compare to cultivars hardy in the United Kingdom, or the southern and western United States, our plants exhibit attractive single red flowers and glossy evergreen foliage and they represent a significant advance in the hardiness of common camellia in

CAMELLIA JAPONICA 'Korean Fire' KNW 352

JOE ZICCARDI

Philadelphia, the mid-Atlantic US and possibly mainland Europe. These plants have great potential for breeding work to improve the hardiness of more ornamental forms of camellia with the potential of growing camellias beyond the 'camellia belts' of the southeast and west coast of the US and the maritime climates of Europe.

Along with evaluating the remaining plants in our collection, over the past several years we have been propagating them and these young plants will be added throughout the Morris Arboretum. Also, cutting-grown plants from the highest rated individuals have been distributed to several other public gardens throughout the northeastern United States. Our hope is that distributing this material will help conserve the germplasm and provide evaluation over a broader range of climates.

Currently we are planning to introduce two or three individual plants from our *Camellia japonica* trials. Where possible we would look forward to sharing this material with gardens and nurserymen in the UK and elsewhere in Europe. Two plants are those that show the highest ratings for combination of habit, foliar quality and flower density. In addition, one individual plant (86-050*Z9/KNW 352) is consistently precocious, regularly blooming in late autumn compared to the normal early spring blooming time of the species. Presently there are a few introductions from the 1984 Korean *Camellia japonica*

CAMELLIA JAPONICA 'Longwood Centennial' KNW 350

TOMASZ ANISKO

collections commercially available. These are: 'Korean Fire' (KNW 352) – a Pennsylvania Horticultural Society Gold Medal Plant Award winner – introduced by Mr Barry Yinger through Hines Nursery (Bensen 2000); 'Longwood Valentine' and 'Longwood Centennial' (KNW 350) introduced by Longwood Gardens (Tomasz Anisko, personal communication).

In summary, after 20 years of evaluation, a number of *Camellia japonica* plants remain at the Morris Arboretum representing some of the most northern collections ever made of common camellia. This evaluation project has fulfilled the Arboretum's plant exploration goals of broadening the genetic pool of known species, extending species hardiness, conserving rare and endangered species and selecting improved horticultural forms.

Anthony S Aiello, Elinor I Goff, Shelley Dillard and Michelle Conners

are curator and director of horticulture, plant recorder, propagator, and curatorial assistant, respectively, at the Morris Arboretum of the University of Pennsylvania. Collectively they curate the Arboretum's living collection of rare and unusual woody plants

Literature Cited ■ Ackerman, WL and Egolf, DR 1991. 'Winter's Rose', 'Snow Flurry' and 'Polar Ice' Camellias. *HortScience* 26: 1432–1433. Ackerman, WL and Egolf DR 1992. 'Winter's Charm', 'Winter's Hope' and 'Winter's Star' Camellias. *HortScience* 27: 855–856. Bensen, SD (ed.) 2000. New Plants for 2001: Shrubs. *American Nurseryman* 192 (12): 34. Dirr, MA, Lindstrom, OM Jr, Lewandowski R and Vehr, MJ 1993. *J. Environ. Hort.* 11 (4): 200–203. Flint, HL 1997. *Landscape Plants for Eastern North America*. (2nd edition. John Wiley and Sons, New York). Meyer, PW 1985. Botanical riches from afar. *Morris Arboretum Newsletter* 14 (1): 4–5. Yinger, B 1989. Plant Trek: In pursuit of a hardy camellia. *Flower and Garden* 33 (2): 104–106.

Francis Hanger – the father of modern rhododendron breeding

COLIN CROSBIE

THE NAME OF FRANCIS HANGER (1901–1961) will be remembered by few apart from an earlier generation of staff and students at Wisley and some in the rhododendron world. The impact of his work on hybridisation still lives on however, especially in his beloved rhododendrons.

FRANCIS HANGER at Wisley (date unknown)

© RHS LINDLEY LIBRARY

Hanger learned his horticultural trade in the typical way, by working for a number of estates and gardens, as well as spending some time as a soldier in the Devonshire regiment. He first came to prominence as head gardener at Exbury, a position he held from 1934 until he moved to RHS Garden Wisley in 1946.

This was one of the great periods to be working in British gardens, with many new plants being introduced from abroad, especially China. Lionel de Rothschild, the owner of Exbury, subscribed to many plant hunting trips by people such as George Forrest and Frank Kingdon Ward. He was developing a large woodland garden, which is still one of the finest in Britain, and in Hanger he had a head gardener who had great vision, a passion and understanding, and a steely determination to succeed. Hanger also became a great show man, and his exhibits at Vincent Square and Chelsea were of the very highest standard and much enjoyed. A strong but friendly rivalry developed between Lord Aberconway's head gardener at Bodnant, North Wales and Hanger as to who would have the greatest success at the RHS Shows.

He had a good eye for selecting plants, especially the best forms of plants grown from wild collected seed and he used this to good advantage when selecting rhododendrons and azaleas for his breeding programme that was taking place at Exbury during this time.

In 1946 Hanger became Curator of RHS Garden Wisley, at a time when many areas of the garden were being developed, especially the area of woodland known as Battleston Hill. Work here had started in 1937, but had stopped during the war. It started in earnest again under Hanger, with the removal of some 200 large trees and 150 stumps. (It is worth noting that, at that time, they did not have the mechanisation that we have now!) Hanger had realised that the acidic Bagshot sand would be ideal for establishing many of the rhododendrons, camellias, magnolias and other woodland plants that he loved. Donations of plants arrived from the great gardens and nurseries, such as Exbury, Bodnant, Charles Williams at Caerhays, from Sunningdale Nurseries and John Barr Stevenson at Tower

Court, many because of the relocation of Rhododendron Trials from Exbury to Wisley.

Hanger continued his rhododendron breeding during his time at Wisley. However, he will always be remembered for showing one plant which would change the face of rhododendron breeding. That plant was *Rhododendron yakushimanum*, which received great acclaim and caused much excitement when it was exhibited at Chelsea in May 1947. It really did steal the show!

First introduced by Lionel de Rothschild to Exbury in 1934, Hanger brought one of the two *R. yakushimanum* plants with him to Wisley. This plant received a First Class Certificate when exhibited at the 1947 show and Hanger described how, when it was planted on Battleston Hill in 1946, it had outgrown the Exbury plant, thanks to a *"liberal supply of spent hops and water"*. When seen at Chelsea, Hanger reported that *"its white flowers commanded appreciation, however, if it had been seen a week earlier, it would have been more beautiful, as the buds of the upstanding compact trusses were rich pink, fading to a pale pink as they developed to be finally pure white when opened"*. The FCC clone is now known as 'Koichiro Wada' after the discerning and highly influential owner of the renowned Hakoneya Nurseries in Japan from where the plant was imported.

Hanger continued with his rhododendron and azalea breeding and his stud book provides a fascinating insight into his methodical approach. From FH1A, *R.* 'Fabia' x 'Romany Chal' which was late sown in February 1947, two seedlings were named. *R.* 'Tensing' received an AM at Chelsea 1953 and *R.* 'Burma Road' was shown at Vincent Square in 1958.

One of his most successful crosses in 1947 was 'Adrian Koster' x *R. litiense* which gave rise to the wonderful yellow 'Moonshine' Group of hybrids and he was without doubt the first person to hybridise with *R. yakushimanum* when, in 1947, he crossed *R. yakushimanum* with *R. dichroanthum*. In subsequent years he crossed *R. yakushimanum* with *R.* 'Beau Brummel', *R. eriogynum*, *R.* 'Naomi', *R.* 'Fabia', *R.* 'Sir F. Moore' and *R.* 'Pilgrim'. Crossing *R.* 'Pilgrim' with *R. yakushimanum* resulted in the cultivar *R.* 'Lady Bowes Lyon' which is still popular today.

Crosses for two of his best *R. yakushimanum* hybrids were made in 1951, *R.* 'Renoir' (*yakushimanum* x 'Pauline') and *R.* 'Tequila Sunrise' (*yakushimanum* x 'Borde Hill').

Hanger favoured primary crosses between species, however, primary hybrids themselves opened doors for interesting possibilities. *R.* 'Beefeater' was a back cross using *R. elliottii* and *R.* 'Fusilier' (a *griersonianum* x *elliottii* hybrid). Hanger quotes the advantages, *"It must be remembered that trusses of R. elliottii are very full with many more flowers per truss than R. griersonianum and when the trees are mated it is highly probable that the resulting hybrid will carry lax trusses with fewer flowers, but back crossing rectifies this fault and improved the colour, making a truly intense red"*.

During this period Hanger was also hybridising with deciduous azaleas. The best plants were named after rivers throughout the British Isles and some are still growing on Battleston Hill today but regrettably, not all. How marvellous it would be if more of Hanger's 'Rivers' could be found and planted there again.

Francis Hanger is very much the father of modern rhododendron breeding. Hybridisers like Peter Cox, David Leach, Hope Findlay at Windsor, Arthur George

RHODODENDRON 'CALDER'

MIKE SLEIGH

at Hydon Nurseries, Waterers, Harkwood Acres, Ken Janeck and Hans Hachmann have all used *R. yakushimanum* to produce compact, floriferous plants with attractive foliage. A trial of *R. yakushimanum* hybrids has recently finished which included over 120 individual hybrids.

Former Wisley students will remember a strict disciplinarian with a strong work ethos, a man

Rhododendrons	Deciduous Azaleas
Arena	**Avon**
Beefeater	Calder
Billy Budd	**Cam**
Biscuit Box	**Cherwell**
Burma Road	**Clyde**
Constable	Dart
Coral Island	**Deben**
Coral Reef	Dee
Degas	Derwent
Eddystone	Deveron
El Greco	**Fal**
Emerald Isle	Frome
Gloriana	Hanger's Flame
Lady Bowes Lyon	**Humber**
Lascaux	**Kensey**
Moonshine	**Liffey**
Moonshine Bright	Medway
Moonshine Crescent	**Mersey**
Moonshine Glow	**Nene**
Moonshine Supreme	**Orwell**
New Comet	**Ribble**
Perfect Lady	**Severn**
Petia	Stour
Pink Ghost	**Tamar**
Raspberry Ripple	Tay
Renoir	**Tees**
Royal Blood	**Thames**
Serena	Trent
Shepherd's Morning	**Tweed**
Telstar	**Tyne**
Tensing	Wansbeck
Tequila Sunrise	**Waveney**
Tosca	**Windrush**
Weybridge	Wye
Wisley Blush	
Wisley Pearl	
Woodcock	

Colin Crosbie is keen to acquire plants or material of those varieties show here in **bold**.

colincrosbie@rhs.org.uk

RHODODENDRON 'TEQUILA SUNRISE' JIM GARDINER

RHODODENDRON 'RENOIR' CLIVE MORRIS

all matters rhododendron and camellia right up until the year of his death in 1961.

In 1939 Hanger was awarded the RHS Associate of Honour, and at 38 he was the youngest ever recipient. In 1953 he received the VMH. His show exhibits were legendary – his 1957 Chelsea exhibit was regarded as one of the best ever seen, with a mossy glade of primula, meconopsis, lilies and of course, rhododendrons.

The next time you admire a *R. yakushimanum* hybrid growing, remember the work done by Hanger many years ago. Even though Battleston Hill at Wisley has changed much since the gales of 1987, its very existence as a woodland garden is largely due to Francis Hanger.

who set and expected high standards in all areas of horticultural work and above all, an outstanding and talented plantsman.

From its rebirth after the war until 1953, he was a member of the Yearbook Editorial Committee, contributing the very first article in 1946 on Exbury Rhododendrons. He remained a regular provider of sage advice and opinion on

Colin Crosbie

is the Superintendent of Woody Plants at RHS Garden Wisley

The threat of *Phytophthora ramorum* to woody plant collections...

IAN WRIGHT

SINCE 2003 A NEW THREAT has appeared in UK gardens, a problem that has yet to be fully understood and one which is potentially very damaging to our woody plant collections – *Phytophthora ramorum* (PR), known in the USA as 'Sudden Oak Death'.

PR is a fungus-like pathogen, belonging to a group of organisms known as the Oomycetes. Until recently they were thought to be fungi as they produce spores, have hyphae and are unable to manufacture their own food but acquire nutrition by degrading and absorbing living plant tissue. DNA analysis in the 1990s indicated that these organisms were more closely related to the algae groups (diatoms and brown algae in particular). They have since been placed in a separate taxonomic Kingdom, Chromista, as opposed to the Kingdom Fungi. Therefore *Phytophthora ramorum* is 'fungus-like'.

Infection with PR will often, but not always induce a host plant to display disease symptoms, but will not necessarily kill it. In biological terms, a 'host' is a living entity (plant or part of a plant) that the pathogen obtains its nutrients from through infection, colonisation and breakdown of the tissues. Symptoms such as death of growing shoots, loss of foliar and bleeding lesions on the bark are characteristic.

PR has a complex lifecycle completed on colonised host plants. It can rapidly reproduce asexually under favourable weather conditions (cool to mild temperature and very high humidity/rain). This type of reproduction only occurs on foliage, fruit and tender shoots of susceptible host plants. When environmental conditions are right many microscopic sporangia, which are lemon-shaped structures, develop on the surface of infected leaves. The contents of each sporangium divide up to form about 20 motile zoospores that are released from the sporangium in wet conditions. Zoospores swim in a thin film of water to healthy host tissue and infect it, thus repeating the cycle. Zoospores are therefore considered the primary form of inoculum (infectious propagules) of PR. Under favourable conditions inoculum can be produced abundantly and rapidly (within hours). This type of inoculum is not formed on the bleeding lesions on tree stems.

PR was first identified along the west coast of the USA in the 1990s where a close relation of the strain of the pathogen affecting the UK is devastating the American tan oak (*Lithocarpus densiflorus*) population along with other native American oak species (*Quercus agrifolia* (Coast live oak) and *Q. kelloggii* for example). The UK and US types of the pathogen are known to be different from each other. The UK population of PR is slightly more aggressive than its American counterpart, grows faster, is more stable and is comprised largely of the A1 Mating Type. The American population is less aggressive than the European population, has slower growth and two main genetic lineages, and is comprised uniquely of the A2 Mating Type. There is great concern that if the American and

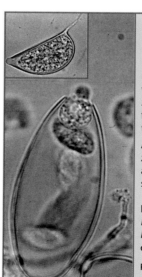

PHYTOPHTHORA RAMORUM
(European lineage, Mating Type A1) mature sporangium with emerging zoospores – the main form of inoculum that drives epidemics

Average diameter of zoospores 8–10µm, average length of sporangia 40–70µm

INSET Sporangium of *Phytophthora kernoviae* for comparison

FOREST RESEARCH

OOSPORE OF *P. RAMORUM* produced artificially as the result of sexual reproduction; not known to occur in nature as *P. ramorum* requires compatible mating strains (A1 and A2) to be in close contact. Average diameter 27–32μm

FOREST RESEARCH

The list of susceptible plants continues to grow and now includes a wide range of woody genera other than *Viburnum* and *Rhododendron*, such as *Magnolia*, *Pieris*, *Drimys* and *Kalmia*; and many tree species, but particularly European beech, are susceptible to this pathogen. Regularly updated lists of susceptible plants in the UK are available on the UK's Department for Environment, Food and Rural Affairs (DEFRA), the EU funded Framework 6 project (RAPRA) and Forest Research and Central Science Laboratory websites.

European populations come into contact with one another they will able to sexually reproduce, creating very long-lived spores called oospores and that the progeny may be even more aggressive than the parent types.

When the disease was first noted in the UK it was identified mainly on viburnums and rhododendrons in nurseries but was later detected on these and other hosts in outdoor situations. The initial concern was – and still is – the potential risk of infection in our own woodlands and native tree species. Since the initial discovery of *Phytophthora ramorum* our understanding of the pathogen has grown and with it our apprehension.

Outbreaks of PR have been fairly widespread within nurseries in the UK, perhaps an indication of how quickly any disease can move when a pathway is available. Many nursery outbreaks, however, have been contained and eradicated successfully, due to the nature of these sites and the vigilance of the UK Plant Health Inspection Service, but it is a more difficult and costly process to control once outside the nursery walls. In the 'outdoor' situation the greatest concentration of outbreaks is in the southwest, including Cornwall and southern Wales, but the epidemic has spread across most parts of England and Wales and has now also been found in Scotland and Northern Ireland.

. . . from a Head Gardener's perspective

Sir Edward Bolitho gave Trengwainton, in southwest Cornwall, to the National Trust in 1961 after he received the Victoria Medal of Honour from the RHS for 'Services to Horticulture'. The skilled work completed earlier in the 1930s by Alfred Creek, the then Head Gardener, helped the garden win national accolades for the new hybrids and material propagated from the 1927–8 Kingdon-Ward expedition to Assam and the Mishmi hills in upper Burma.

During the last 6 years, as the current Head Gardener at Trengwainton, I have had many concerns about factors affecting our ageing plant collection. Honey Fungus (*Armillaria* spp.) in particular causes endless heartache as a result of the annual losses it causes. *Phytophthora ramorum* and the more recently discovered *Phytophthora*

***MAGNOLIA CAMPBELLII*,** planted in 1926 at Trengwainton and as yet uninfected IAN WRIGHT

PHYTOPHTHORA RAMORUM on *Rhododendron* 'Loderi King George'   IAN WRIGHT

leaved species such as *R. sinogrande* could also be susceptible. Susceptibility testing is now being carried out on a wide range of *Rhododendron* species. Obviously the threat to our own Trengwainton hybrids is causing us the greatest concern.

Various symptoms have been observed such as dying leaf midribs, leaves and shoots with drought-like characteristics, wet-looking fungal blotches on leaves, dead flower buds and canker lesions on stems. With smaller plants we have found that the disease will usually overwhelm the plant, defoliating then eventually killing it. Larger plants seem to struggle on, with the risk that they will succumb to a secondary disease in their weakened condition. We have found some types will temporarily shows signs of recovery, only to present with new symptoms up to 8 months later, perhaps due to weather conditions – a point I will return to later.

One of the major hosts of the disease was found to be *Rhododendron ponticum*, its huge biomass providing a host for large inoculum levels. As with other gardens in Cornwall, we are removing *R. ponticum* where possible within the garden as well as from the immediate

kernoviae have now given us additional cause for concern. (Found while surveying for *P. ramorum*, *P. kernoviae* is, at the moment, predominantly Cornwall-based, as its name suggests [Kernow being the Cornish word for Cornwall]. However, scientists regard it as a more aggressive strain.)

Although our collection of plants has declined in content over the last few decades, it is still acknowledged as being of significant merit both within the National Trust and beyond.

Against that background, we made a decision not to sit back and wait any longer for further damage from these or any other diseases, but to try to react proactively, identifying ways of safeguarding our collections, as well as working with others to understand the disease and manage our gardens to lessen any risk. As a result, we have looked at ways we can help affected gardens and share any good practice we learn both internally and externally.

RHODODENDRONS

Outbreaks of PR & PK have mainly been identified on the medium to smaller leaved types such as *R.* 'Fragrantissimum', *R.* 'Golden Oriole', *R.* 'Temple Belle' and the various *R. ponticum* hybrids. However there are cases on the 'Loderi' types and the risk that some of the larger

PHYTOPHTHORA KERNOVIAE on *Rhododendron* 'Ding Dong' – a Trengwainton hybrid

IAN WRIGHT

MAGNOLIA DELAVAYI infected with *Phytophthora kernoviae*

IAN WRIGHT

surrounding area, in order to lessen the risk to our more valuable specimens. This brings additional problems however, as a lot of the older *ponticums* were planted for shelter and indeed, like other collections, ours includes a lot of *ponticum* hybrids.

MAGNOLIAS

A wide range of our *Magnolia* species have proved positive with both of the diseases, for example *Magnolia delavayi*, *M. salicifolia* and *M.* x *soulangeana* to name but a few.

A mature *Magnolia delavayi* with *Phytophthora kernoviae*, at over 10 metres in height with a large canopy, growing in a free standing and open situation, displayed similar characteristics to some of the infected rhododendrons when it began dropping green leaves with dying lower midribs. (A sign that always raises suspicion that there may be a problem is a carpet of green leaves under a 'susceptible' evergreen plant.) As spring turned to summer, the leaf drop stopped, but resumed in the autumn. This tree has now lost around 20% of its canopy and is obviously now in a much weakened state and potentially more at risk from secondary diseases. Moreover, rain dripping from it, carrying inoculum picked up from running over infected leaf surfaces, has also killed a young *Rhododendron* 'Morvah' (a Trengwainton hybrid) growing beneath its canopy.

The trunk of the *M. delavayi* has also developed a bleeding lesion on its bark – a dark residue

seeping from spots on the stems – which is an indication of infection within the growing cambium and inner bark. In general, symptoms that can be seen on the outside of a tree are indicative of only 5% of the infection beneath the bark's surface.

Similar foliar symptoms have been observed on mature plants of *M. salicifolia*. As with rhododendrons, the disease seems to come and go, depending on weather conditions.

CAMELLIAS

Camellias seem to be slightly more resistant to the disease when mature, but not when in a nursery situation. Perhaps some resistance is gained from the thicker, glossy leaves, but one should not be complacent as, if a high level of inoculum is nearby, positive cases will almost certainly be found on mature plants, and defoliation is sure to follow.

ONGOING RESEARCH

The Central Science Laboratory (CSL, York) and Forest Research (Alice Holt Lodge, Surrey) are currently undertaking various research projects to understand the disease, and a gradual picture of the cycle of the pathogen is emerging.

PHYTOPHTHORA RAMORUM causing defoliation on *Camellia* x *williamsii* 'Donation'

IAN WRIGHT

RHODODENDRON 'Morvah' at Trengwainton

IAN WRIGHT

ON-SITE IDENTIFICATION AND ANALYSIS

At present a Lateral Flow Device (LFD) is used to confirm the presence of any of the *Phytophthora* species on plant material. If the test proves positive, a sample is sent to the laboratory to test if it is in fact either *P. ramorum* or *P. kernoviae*. This process can take 10 days.

New methods are being trialled to reduce the test time and increase the identification success rate. One new system is called a Polymerase Chain Reaction (PCR) or 'Smart Cycler' which uses a magnetic process to capture clean DNA. This is then tested against known results and controls to ascertain whether the disease is either *P. ramorum* or *P. kernoviae*. This process can provide an answer in around two hours and can be used on site.

Another area of research uses laser and digital imagery to create a 3D picture and monitors how the disease spreads once a plant has become infected.

Sensors at affected sites are also monitoring temperature and check air samples for the presence of airborne *P. ramorum* or *P. kernoviae* spores.

Known pathogen-free leaves of 'susceptible' species of *Magnolia* or *Rhododendron* are used as 'bait' and placed in watercourses to establish if the water is positive for PR and/or PK.

THE INFLUENCE OF THE CLIMATE

The possibility of a link with climatic conditions is another area for research. The disease does seem to be more active in warm, wet conditions (not good news for areas with high rainfall) and become less visible in hot, dry periods such as the summer of 2006.

One can predict a resurgence of the disease to within a few days, usually around 10 days or so after a wet period starts in the spring or autumn. However Cornwall's winters are generally mild and damp and positive results have continued to be picked up throughout the season.

A PROACTIVE RESPONSE

If you don't know what a plant is, then how can you quantify its historical and genetic significance?

SURVEYING

At Trengwainton, we found we needed a more comprehensive set of records than we had assumed were in place, with large areas of our collection being left out of the Woody Plant Catalogue system we had been using. The Catalogue was very out of date, the situation being accentuated by the quick turnover of plants in this area of the country. We needed a better picture of what we were looking after and growing in our garden.

RHODODENDRON 'Johnnie Johnston' at Trengwainton

PAM HAYWARD

Using the new NT plant database, we have completed around 75% of a full survey and input this to the system. This essential knowledge has enabled us to form a Priority Propagation List of the most historically valuable specimens on the property. We can now instigate a programme to safeguard these plants before we sustain further losses.

A future aim would be to use a GPS system to digitally map the collection, in conjunction with a programme of fixed point photography and we will also be revisiting our conservation plan for the garden to include ideas for temporary planting to fill areas where losses have occurred.

HYGIENE
The threat from the disease has also made us review our general garden hygiene. Working from plant to plant within a garden situation can potentially spread this or indeed any disease.

Various disinfectants are suggested for use; obviously the stronger the product, the more risk to the operator and the more restrictions from government regulations, even though in most cases these products will only form a barrier, not kill the disease. Washing tools and boots etc. on a regular basis is recommended and this good practice should become force of habit.

Sweeping up and burning fallen diseased leaves is also essential to help keep inoculum levels down.

Being a garden open to the public, we are satisfied that there is little risk of spread from visitors to our garden. The normal requests we make of any visitor, for example: keeping to the paths, dogs on leads and non-removal of plant material should significantly lessen any risk. We have also stepped up our path cleaning maintenance operation.

Initial trials are underway with a chemical called phosphonate which may, in the future, offer some protection to historic plant material. However, this is very much in the preliminary stages of trial and research.

PROPAGATION
When the disease is confirmed within the boundaries of a garden it becomes more difficult to employ some standard plant propagation options due to the risk of spreading the disease by the movement of untested green material, for example.

We also discovered we had been watering young replacement plants in our garden nursery with water which has since been tested *P. ramorum* positive.

RHODODENDRON 'Morvah' plantlets in the Duchy College Micropropropagation Unit   IAN WRIGHT

The traditional propagation procedure within the National Trust is via the central Plant Conservation Programme nursery located at Knightshayes in Devon, but this route is difficult when infection is confirmed. We have consequently been working with Duchy College at Rosewarne in Cornwall to micropropagate our more valuable specimens. (Micropropagation is the production of a potentially infinite number of plants by using bud or shoot tissue in a controlled solution usually within a laboratory type situation.) So far, they have had considerable success in encouraging buds to respond to the process within laboratory conditions and it is hoped that, once growing, the infection-free material could itself be propagated and then passed on to Knightshayes. In an ideal situation we would hope that enough plants are produced to distribute to other clean gardens with similar growing conditions to our own. The micropropagation unit has achieved a good success rate with our Trengwainton rhodo-dendron hybrids such as 'Morvah', 'Creeks Cross' and 'Johnnie Johnston'.

Buds from both *Magnolia delavayi* and *M. campbellii* ssp. *mollicomata* have also shown initial signs of response. We remain hopeful that our number one priority plant, *Rhododendron macabeanum*, will in time respond to this process. *R. macabeanum* KW7724 flowered for the first time at Trengwainton from material brought back by Frank Kingdon-Ward from his plant hunting expeditions to Assam and the Mishmi Hills in upper Burma in 1927–8. It was awarded a First Class Certificate from the RHS in 1938.

THE MICROPROP PROCESS

Plants are cultured in an agar jelly containing specific nutrients and hormones, specially formulated to be appropriate to the material type and the desired result i.e. whether it is intended to increase numbers through shoot generation/multiplication or rooting. Samples are first disinfected to remove any competing or parasitic microbes, like bacteria and fungi which are detrimental to the plant. This is achieved by using a surface sterilant – usually a hypochlorous solution or alcohol. The action of these is enhanced by the addition of wetting agents which improve surface contact with the sterilant. The process often involves multiple stages with various concentrations and treatments.

Once samples are clean and shoot multiplication has been stimulated, the number of plants can increase exponentially. Micropropagation is typically used for commercial propagation on a large scale, but the same methods can also be used to multiply rare and threatened plants.

The technique of micropropagation has many merits when dealing with plant pathogens such as *P. ramorum*. Firstly, one can produce a large number of plants from a small quantity of parent material and, once established, continue to produce them as required. Secondly, it provides a high degree of confidence in pathogen elimination in the optimum growth conditions which are provided. Any infection rapidly multiplies to the point where the colony is visible and if no contamination is observed after an extended period the assumption can be made that decontamination was successful.

Some problems with the process still remain such as:

DECONTAMINATION

Plant material, which has matured *in vivo*, is typically unsuitable for micropropagation since total decontamination is virtually impossible. It doesn't take long in the outside world for a sample to become riddled with fungal spores, algae and bacteria. This is especially relevant in the protected microclimates that occur in the old walled gardens at Trengwainton where many of these varieties are planted. Unfortunately, without clean stock plants, this is the only propagation material available for much of the year. To sufficiently clean even very young material may require a concentration of sterilant so high it may prove phytotoxic.

CULTIVAR VARIATION

The wide variation between cultivars means that a treatment that has produced significant results with one sample may have absolutely no effect on another. This makes it difficult to produce a definitive protocol for propagation because of varying responses. Paradoxically however, it isn't a viable proposition to produce a different protocol for each cultivar because then the methods are too complex to replicate.

OXIDISATION

A problem found with camellias is that damaged tissue oxidises (seals over) very readily. This then inhibits water and nutrient uptake, and some of the exudates (natural sealants) can even cause the tissue to degrade.

SLOW GROWTH RATE

Ancient plants often demonstrate a gradual decrease in vigour as they age, so the rate of growth in material taken from a plant of 10–20 years old is considerable when compared to samples taken from plants aged over 150 years.

A WAKE-UP CALL

P. ramorum is proving to be a significant 'wake-up call' for our gardens and although one could argue that if it does prove to be 'just another problem that we have to live with', there might just as easily be another disease, pest or extreme weather condition awaiting its turn in the future.

There is a continuous danger of introducing new pathogens into our gardens when we bring in exotic plants or nursery plants produced in different countries where they may have been exposed to alien pests and microbes. We will need to reassess how we are to maintain the beauty and variety in our gardens without threatening our current collections.

By evaluating the management of our garden and plant collection, the changing climate and the seemingly endless stream of new pests and diseases, and also taking into consideration the resource level and our evolving roles, it is apparent that ideally we need to spend more time giving the ageing plants within the collection the annual care they need, i.e. mulching, pruning or feeding, especially since the health of some of the collection has been compromised by the loss of canopy cover after the two storms of 1987 and 1990. It has made us look more closely into our aftercare of young plants and made sure we continue to rejuvenate and propagate our older, historically-valuable specimens. I firmly believe in the old analogy that healthy plants would stand a better chance if threatened by *Phytophthora*, or any other disease. We will certainly plant less and look after more in the future.

Further, more detailed information on PR and PK can be found on the following websites:
www.defra.gov.uk/planth/pramorum.htm
www.forestry.gov.uk
www.rapra.csl.gov.uk

email: planthealth.info@defra.gsi.gov.uk

With thanks to Sandra Denman from Forest Research and Peter Hodgson from Duchy College for their help with the sections on PR and PK, and micropropagation respectively.

Ian Wright
is Head Gardener at Trengwainton and Gardens Adviser to The National Trust Devon & Cornwall

---

We would be grateful if anybody has reference to, or has living material of, the following rhododendrons that we believe were originally bred or raised at Trengwainton.

'Beta' A selection from *R. lanigerum* KW8251; Bolitho 1963; rose-opal.

'Bulldog' (*elliottii* x 'Earl of Athlone'); Bolitho 1937; deep red.

'Cherubim' (*Azma* x *elliottii*); Bolitho 1943.

'Cornish Cream' (*campylocarpum* x *Fortorb*); Bolitho 1937.

'Cornish Glow' (Lanarth hybrid x Lanarth hybrid); Bolitho 1947; crimson changing to orange yellow.

'Ding Dong' (*fortunei* ssp. *discolor* x *lacteum*); Bolitho pre 1958; white.

'Johnnie Johnston' (*johnstoneanum* (double form) x *tephropeplum*); Bolitho pre 1958 – we need to bulk up our few remaining specimens.

'Laerdal' (*johnstoneanum* x *dalhousiae*); Bolitho 1937; pure white.

'Lal Kapra' (*neriiflorum* x *sanguineum*); Bolitho 1958; red.

'Lanyon' (*haematodes* x *elliottii*); Bolitho pre 1958.

'Miss Pink' (Azma Group x *griersonianum*); Bolitho 1943.

'Morvah' (*elliottii* x *wattii*); Bolitho pre 1956; turkey red.

'Nanceglos' (*elliottii* x *fortunei*); Bolitho 1945.

'Penalverne' ('Earl of Athlone' x *griersonianum*); Bolitho pre 1958.

'Penhale' (*fortunei* x *facetum*); Bolitho 1945.

'Rubeotinctum' A selection from *R. johnstoneanum* KW7732; Bolitho 1941; white with a deep pink stripe on each lobe and a pink or yellow blotch.

Trengwainton, PENZANCE, Cornwall TR20 8SA

ian.wright@national trust.org.uk

KALMIAS – American Beauties

ALAN PULLEN

FEW HARDY EVERGREEN SHRUBS equal kalmias for their exquisite charm, especially *Kalmia latifolia*, with its exquisitely crimped, glistening pink buds held in large terminal corymbs opening in June to light pink saucer-shaped flowers with purple spots around the anther pockets, each bloom resembling a tiny parasol. Yet, in spite of their appeal, they are still relatively unfamiliar to many gardeners in Britain.

This small group of shrubs (there are just seven species in this North American genus) has a geographic range extending from Newfoundland to western Cuba on the eastern side of the continent and from Central California through the Rocky Mountains to the Yukon on the west coast. The genus is now regarded as a relatively primitive member of the *Ericaceae* and has been placed in the sub-family *Ericoideae*. The most distinctive feature of the *Kalmia* genus is its pollen-discharge mechanism. Near the middle of the corolla are ten pouches forming small lobes on each ridge of the flower bud. Just before the bud opens, the elongating filaments push the anthers upward and into the pouches (*see below*). As the corolla opens, the elastic filaments bend backward under tension causing the anthers to be held in the pouches and forced down and outward. When the flower is disturbed by a large insect, one or more of the anthers are released from their pouches. The freed filament snaps the anther upward, showering the insect with pollen. Bumblebees (*Bombus* spp) are the usual insects to visit kalmia flowers and when searching around the base of the corolla, the insect's proboscis 'liberates' the stamens, projecting pollen on to the underside of its body. This pollen is then rubbed on to the

KALMIA LATIFOLIA 'Snowdrift' (*note position of anthers*)   MICHAEL SHUTTLEWORTH

stigmas of subsequently visited flowers. Honeybees (*Apis* spp) rarely, if ever, visit kalmias.

In the USA, kalmias are commonly referred to as laurels, a name derived from colonial times when the early colonists likened the foliage to that of the European Sweet Bay – *Laurus nobilis*. The common name of most species has the suffix 'laurel' with the first part of the name usually being a descriptive reference to its native habitat, e.g. mountain laurel, eastern bog laurel, western alpine laurel etc.

The generic name is after the Finnish botanist Pehr Kalm (1716–1779), a student of Linnaeus, who was sent out to the New World in 1748 by the Swedish Academy of Science to obtain seeds of plants that would thrive in the Swedish climate and soil. Kalm spent three years in the New World, his explorations extending from Pennsylvania, through New York and New Jersey, into southern Canada. A shrewd observer, his detailed studies of mountain laurel (the popular name of the species *K. latifolia*) and other genera were described in his journal, published on his return to Europe. Mountain laurels were common in colonial gardens when Kalm arrived in the New World. The American born botanist, John Bartram (1699–1777), founder of the first American Botanic Garden in Philadelphia, had sent living plants of *K. latifolia* in 1734 and *K. angustifolia* two years later, to Peter Collinson, a London draper, who planted seeds and plants he obtained from his many American business correspondents in his garden in Mill Hill, now part of Mill Hill School, London. Another recipient of living plants from Bartram was the Hon. Charles Hamilton (1704–1786) who planted the many plants he received, including kalmias, in his garden at Painshill, Cobham, Surrey. This garden has now been restored by the Painshill Trust who hold the NCCPG National Plant Heritage Collection® of John Bartram introductions. Mark Catesby (1683–1749) reported in 1743 that *K. latifolia* from Pennsylvania had flowered in his garden in Fulham in 1740.

KALMIA LATIFOLIA in its native habitat, Lexington, South Carolina USA

MIKE CREEL

KALMIA LATIFOLIA –
THE MOUNTAIN LAUREL

The common species, *K. latifolia*, is native to the eastern United States, distributed particularly throughout the Allegheny and Appalachian Mountains, where it is usually found growing on the dry, rocky slopes and clearings as an understory shrub, often on acid, sandy soils, a good indication of its soil requirements in cultivation. (In Britain, kalmias generally thrive better in the drier eastern counties, providing the soil moisture is maintained by adequate mulching after winter rainfall.) Some natural habitats are often near the coast, but kalmias will not tolerate salt-laden air. In cultivation, this usually tall, well-branched shrub rarely achieves its ultimate 3.75m in height. The leaves are alternate, elliptic, dark green above and light green below and pleasantly petioled. The leaves are very ornamental in themselves, the attractive foliage creating a splendid setting for the gorgeous blooms which often obscure the plant's foliage with the great wealth of blossom.

The National Plant Collection of *Kalmia latifolia* AGM, its cultivars and forms was established in 1987 at Secretts Garden Centre, Surrey, in new display gardens on land that had formerly been part of the company's extensive market garden. The initial planting was with a fairly intensive grouping of other young trees and shrubs to provide a light canopy for shade and shelter. This canopy was subsequently reduced or thinned to allow for more light and air. The soil is Bargate sand over Lower Greensand with a pH of 6.5, which approximates fairly well to many of the soils in the American habitats where *Kalmia* is found. Composted bark is used when planting, with a bark mulch to help conserve soil moisture. Seaweed based foliar sprays are applied before and again after flowering.

The mountain laurel (also known as the Calico Bush), *K. latifolia*, and its numerous cultivars, generally have pink buds and flowers

with faint spots near the anthers. Variations include both white-flowered and red budded cultivars where the intense bud colour contrasts with the open blooms.

Several of the earliest colour selections originated from the UK. In the 1950s AG Soames introduced a number of cultivars from Sheffield Park, Sussex, including 'Splendens', 'Sheffield Park' and 'Clementine Churchill', which received the RHS Award of Merit in 1952. Following these selections most new cultivars were selected and introduced from the United States. Foremost in selecting and naming new cultivars was Dr RA Jaynes, who for 25 years worked as a plant breeder and horticulturist at the Connecticut Agriculture Experiment Station, continuing his innovative work with kalmias at Broken Arrow Nursery, Hamden, Connecticut which he established in

KALMIA LATIFOLIA 'Pink Surprise'
MICHAEL SHUTTLEWORTH

1984. Other notable kalmia breeders in the United States were the late John Eichelser and the late Edmund Mezitt. Their respective families have continued working with kalmias. More recently, some very exciting kalmia hybridising has been carried out by Dr Karl-Heinz Hubbers in Germany, a project which is

KALMIA LATIFOLIA 'Sarah'   MICHAEL SHUTTLEWORTH

pink. Another to be recommended is 'Snowdrift'. An unusual white selection is 'Shooting Star'– a single recessive gene giving this rarely seen cultivar its distinctive flower shape with a corolla cut into five lobes that reflex when open.

The banded mountain laurel, *K. latifolia* f. *fuscata*, has flowers that are pigmented and marked with a maroon or cinnamon band inside the corolla. Noteworthy cultivars include 'Carousel', with an intricate pattern of purplish-cinnamon and heavy pigmentation on open flowers; 'Freckles' AGM, with light pink buds and open flowers which have ten purplish spots above each of the ten anther pouches, and 'Peppermint', with a maroon-red pigmentation on open flowers, a ten-spoked star radiating from the base of the corolla, all on a near white ground. Finally, two more *fuscata* gems: 'Pinwheel', with pink tinged buds and open flowers, which

very much ongoing. Dr Jaynes has recently retired as the International Registration Authority for Kalmias, a role now taken on by Highstead Arboretum at Redding, Connecticut, which currently holds 80 cultivars and forms in its collection.

Outstanding pink bud cultivars include 'Pink Charm' AGM, with deep pink buds opening to rich pink blooms; 'Pink Frost', with large flowers of frosty, blush pink; 'Pink Star', where the corolla is deeply cut to form large, star-shaped flowers of clear pink and 'Pink Surprise' with strong pink buds opening to a medium pink. Among the red budded cultivars, 'Ostbo Red', the first named red bud, is still a favourite for the brilliance of its colour. Other eye-catching red buds include 'Clementine Churchill' AM, with flowers of Tyrian rose on the outside of the corolla and rose-madder on the inside; 'Heart of Fire', a seedling of 'Ostbo Red' having wide-open blooms of deep pink; 'Olympic Fire' AGM, another outstanding 'Ostbo Red' seedling; 'Raspberry Glow' with flower buds of deep burgundy red opening to strong pink and the eye-catching and intensely coloured 'Sarah'.

There are a few excellent white-flowered cultivars and one of the best is 'Pristine', selected from a natural population in South Carolina for its compact habit and pure, crystalline white flowers that lack any trace of

KALMIA LATIFOLIA 'Galaxy'

MICHAEL SHUTTLEWORTH

are almost filled with cinnamon-maroon pigment, with the centre and scalloped edge white. The colouring of the flower truss resembles the flowers of sweet william (*Dianthus barbatus*). The exciting cultivar 'Galaxy' is the first named selection to combine the near-petaled flower form with the burgundy inner colour of the f. *fuscata* forms. The corolla opens wide, with five deeply pigmented petal-like lobes edged with white.

The miniature mountain laurel, *Kalmia latifolia* f. *myrtifolia*, is characterised by smaller leaves and compact growth. Cultivars in this group include 'Elf', with pale pink buds and near white flowers; 'Little Linda' AGM, the first

to be garden worthy plants and are available from specialist nurseries and some plant centres.

KALMIA ANGUSTIFOLIA VAR. ANGUSTIFOLIA F. RUBRA AGM – THE SHEEP LAUREL

This desirable form of sheep laurel has deep rosy-red flowers carried in axillary or terminal corymbs with individual flowers 1cm across. This stoloniferous shrub is about 1m tall and flowers over a long period from mid-May and through June. Cultivation is the same as *K. latifolia*.

Kalmia angustifolia var. *angustifolia* f. *candida* is an excellent white-flowered form with light green foliage and is well worth seeking out.

KALMIA LATIFOLIA F. MYRTIFOLIA 'Elf'

MICHAEL SHUTTLEWORTH

named cultivar to combine the miniature habit of f. *myrtifolia* with red budded flowers and 'Minuet' which has light pink buds but with open flowers banded with bright cinnamon as in f. *fuscata*. The botanical form of f. *myrtifolia* is rarely found in the wild and is now produced as a cultivar. The buds are light pink opening to white flowers making it very attractive.

The other species in this lovely genus have flowers which are generally less spectacular than those of *K. latifolia*, nevertheless, they each have their own unique charm. I have chosen a representative selection, most of which I consider

KALMIA MICROPHYLLA – THE ALPINE LAUREL

The only species of the genus found west of the Rocky Mountains. This charming, diminutive species grows to about 7.5cm tall. This is an excellent plant for growing in the peat garden or in a pocket of acid soil in a rock garden. A neat, attractive little plant with tiny rose-purple flowers, it is a real gem.

KALMIA CUNEATA – WHITE WICKY

One of the rarest shrubs in the USA, *K. cuneata* is found in only a few locations in southeastern North Carolina and South Carolina. A many-branched, erect growing shrub up to 1.5m tall with alternate, oblong-obovate deciduous leaves and white flowers, 1.5cm across and borne in umbellate corymbs from the leaf axils of the preceding year. Flowering in early spring before new foliage and shoots expand and best suited to moist soil.

KALMIA POLIFOLIA – THE EASTERN BOG LAUREL

As the common name suggests, this species is well suited for planting in very moist soil, perhaps as a pond side feature. A wiry, slender-stemmed shrub with terminal clusters of rose-purple flowers, it grows to about 90cm and is usually earlier to flower than the other species. In very wet soil it can form dense mats of growth.

Kalmia polifolia f. leucantha is a delightful white-flowered dwarf form with light green foliage and a compact habit which was found in a single location in Newfoundland. Another dwarf form from this province is K. polifolia Newfoundland form with the same rose-purple flowers as the species.

KALMIA HIRSUTA – THE SANDHILL LAUREL

This species has a relatively limited distribution in the wild, occurring along the coastal plain in the southeastern USA. A low-growing shrub 60cm tall, with leaves and stems covered with dense hairs. The solitary, light pink flowers with red markings are borne in the leaf axils. A somewhat difficult species for gardens in Britain.

KALMIA ERICOIDES – THE CUBAN LAUREL

This last species in the genus is endemic to the savannahs of western Cuba; this sparse-branched shrub to 90cm tall with pink flowers is unsuitable for British gardens.

KALMIA ANGUSTIFOLIA **F. RUBRA (ABOVE) AND** *KALMIA CUNEATA* **(RIGHT)** at the National Kalmia Collection at Secretts Garden Centre, Godalming, Surrey

MICHAEL SHUTTLEWORTH

Kalmias associate well with azaleas, rhododendrons and many other ericaceous plants requiring similar soil and growing conditions. They have a greater tolerance of drought than most rhododendrons and, with the ever more apparent effects of global

KALMIAS FRAME THE VIEW in this perfect plant association at the National Plant Collection

MICHAEL SHUTTLEWORTH

warming, this could prove invaluable. They look particularly good when planted in the company of *Cornus florida* cvs. which come into flower just before them and with *Cornus kousa* cvs. which flower at the same time as them or just after, thus extending the overall scene. Other complementary small trees to consider for background structure include *Acer palmatum* cvs., *Amelanchier*, *Oxydendrum arboreum* and *Stewartia*, companions which would also enhance the scene with autumn colours. Flowering shrubs which might be considered include *Aronia melanocarpa*, *Calycanthus floridus* and *Hydrangea quercifolia* which would also give autumn colour. Finally, there is a wealth of ground cover plants and evergreen or herbaceous infill perennials such as *Cornus canadensis* AGM, *Epimedium*, ferns, *Heuchera*, hostas, *Pachysandra*, *Tellima* and *Tiarella*, not to mention such early spring delights as *Anemone nemorosa* 'Robinsoniana' AGM, *Erythronium*, hardy cyclamen and trilliums.

All these plants, in the company of the lovely *Kalmia* will provide a garden of lasting joy and colour to match any.

Alan Pullen

is Custodian of the NCCPG National Plant Collection of Kalmia latifolia *at Secretts Garden Centre, Godalming, Surrey*

Magnolia sargentiana and *Magnolia dawsoniana*: Exploration and field surveys in the Dafengding of southern Sichuan

PETER WHARTON

A YOUNG 13M *MAGNOLIA SARGENTIANA* with a clear stem and characteristically upright crown near Gudui village, Leibo – Mamize Nature Reserve, s. Sichuan. The coppiced and now regenerating forest on the hillside beyond the cultivated valley-bottom contains Sargent's magnolia

PETER WHARTON

TWO SUPERB MAGNOLIAS – *Magnolia sargentiana* and *M. dawsoniana* – have played a major role in western horticulture since their discovery by Ernest Henry Wilson in 1908 during the 'Golden Age' of Chinese plant discovery. The lion's-share of these magnolias growing in our private and public gardens is derived from these early Wilson collections, many from vegetative propagations, but most from open pollinated seed. The risk of genetic contamination from garden-collected seed has

not been universally understood, but is now becoming widely acknowledged. It is increasingly clear that we need to 'horticulturally reconnect' with the wild plants if we are to distinguish them and appreciate their genuine attributes. The true status of these species is only now being revealed. In this account I will provide an overview of recent observations I have made in the wild against the background of efforts by both Chinese and international organizations to promote and assist *in situ* conservation.

My personal interest in these two species has been further stimulated by the recently published *The Red List of Magnoliaceae* (Cicuzza *et al*, 2007), which highlights many of the challenges that lie ahead in conserving the habitat of so many threatened species worldwide. This is the first global assessment of the conservation status of *Magnoliaceae*. It underlines the lack of detailed field-based information on geographical distribution and the ecology of these species in the wild. *The Red List* is a landmark document, calling for comprehensive collaborative action to conserve these flagship species and the forest ecosystems that support them. This is the context of my work in western China: to assist our Chinese colleagues in 'holding the ground' where these magnificent trees grow.

My formative forestry and arboricultural training in the UK in the 1970s quickly made me aware of these two ephemeral and precocious spring flowering species. They often contribute to the spectacular early spring displays of many British woodland gardens. Botanical travel in China has improved immeasurably since the 1980s. Now internal transportation allows unprecedented acces-sibility to once remote corners of the Celestial Empire, allowing us to extract answers to age-long questions regarding all

MAGNOLIA SARGENTIANA (var. *robusta* of hort. cult). Cultivated plant, UBC Botanical Garden, Vancouver   PETER WHARTON

manner of botanical mysteries. These two iconic magnolia taxa are prime targets for this type of investigation. We presently grow in western cultivation a very narrow band of genetic variance within our cultivated plants. Just how few plants were propagated from these Wilsonian collections at the Arnold Arboretum is well illustrated by the comments of the director, Professor Charles S Sargent. On 3 July 1913, he wrote to Leon Chenault of Chenault's nurseries in Orleans, France: "*I want to consult you about Wilson's Chinese Magnolias. We have now only a few plants of these, ...*". He was referring not only to *Magnolia dawsoniana* and *M. sargentiana*, but also *M. sargentiana* var. *robusta* (now placed within *M. sargentiana*). The part Leon Chenault played, in the ultimate successful introduction of these species into the UK is described in detail by Neil G. Treseder (1978, pp.102–103). I have always been bothered by the lack of new introductions of these species from known wild origin. Similarly, our vague understanding of their natural distribution in western China has also introduced a further level of curiosity.

Were these species as rare and imperiled as the literature suggested?

In 2005 I had the good fortune to come into contact with Professor Tang Ya of Sichuan University, through colleagues working in several North American botanical institutions belonging to the North American Consortium for Plant Exploration in China (NACPEC). NACPEC has helped Professor Tang Ya and his students to complete a number of botanical surveys in western Sichuan in the last few years. Professor Tang is head of the Biodiversity and Environmental Studies Laboratory, Sichuan University in Chengdu. It quickly became clear after initial correspondence that we had many ideas and objectives in common. At the general level, botanical field surveys and urgent biodiversity conservation goals were high on our collective minds. In addition, some specific lines of enquiry began to emerge including a host of questions and uncertainties relating to the status of two taxa, *Magnolia dawsoniana* and *Magnolia sargentiana* of southern Sichuan. We began to zero-in on the Dafengding region, which lies 300km southwest of Chengdu, 130km from the sacred Emei Shan (Omei Shan). This region lies in the Xiaoliangshan, to the east of the Huangmaogeng, an extensive complex of ranges that face the moist Red Basin. The wet climate here supports remnants of a once extensive humid evergreen

MAGNOLIA DAWSONIANA. Cultivated plant, UBC Botanical Garden, Vancouver

PETER WHARTON

broadleaved forest. The renowned botanists TT Yu and ZT Guan did some preliminary botanical survey work in the 1930s and from the late 1950s to the early 1960s, yet little else has been undertaken recently, other than some animal and bird investigations. Professor Tang pointed out a group of county, provincial and national nature reserves in Meigu, Mabian, Ebian, Ganluo and Yuexi counties within the Dafengding and these areas became the focus for our field investigations that took place during September 2006.

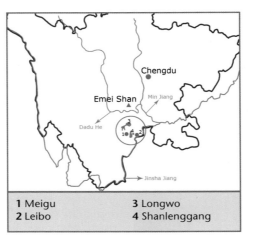

1 Meigu
2 Leibo
3 Longwo
4 Shanlenggang

Professor Tang and I were accompanied in the field by Dr Koen Camelbeke, Director of the Wespelaar Arboretum, Belgium, who proved to be a fine friend and botanical explorer. We were also joined by three of Professor Tang's enthusiastic graduate students, Gao Hui, Wang Jing and Zhang Liyun. Dr. Camelbeke and I rendezvoused at the main Sichuan University campus in the centre of Chengdu. Chengdu, the provincial capital, is situated in the agriculturally rich Red Basin, which is often referred to as the 'Land of Abundance'. The university is a leafy, tree dominated campus with an 'Ivy League' feel about it, as the older brick buildings date back to the 1920s. It is the oldest of three separate Sichuan University campuses in Chengdu, coping with a total student population of over 60,000! Here we met our Chinese colleagues and went over the itinerary for our expedition.

The following day, cloudy, dry weather followed us south. At Ebian we drove westwards and entered the spectacular gorge of the Dadu He (Dadu River). The gorge is cut periodically by slot-like canyons and sadly, punctuated by massive hydroelectric construction. Typical of the many spectacular river valleys of western China was the presence of hard leaved sclerophytic (drought tolerant, evergreen plants) vegetation and crags bereft of any plant life. The arid conditions continued as we turned south along the Yuexi He towards the mining centers of Ganluo and Yuexi. Here vanadium, zinc and, to a lesser degree, coal are extracted from the local mountains. Our goal this day was the small rural town of Longwo, located on the edge of the Meigu – Dafengding National Nature Reserve (MDNNR), the headwaters of the Mabian He. Here we suspected good remnants of the original forest cover could still be found. This is a centre of the Yi minority, an ethnic group known for their animist beliefs and probably why this region still possesses some intact primary forests. We entered the drainage basin of the Mabian He from the west over a pass at 2685m that was shrouded in flying mist. Here we saw the results of extensive past logging – a somber scene of huge blackened stumps of *Abies fabri*, which dotted a grazed

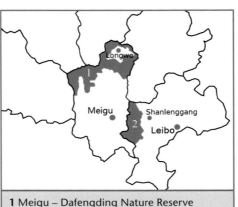

1 Meigu – Dafengding Nature Reserve
2 Leibo – Mamize Nature Reserve

landscape with islands of regeneration. Our spirits were soon uplifted though when we began to see what appeared to be *Magnolia dawsoniana*. There were several freestanding young trees to 7m tall. Others, though previously heavily coppiced, were growing vigorously. Unfortunately, we could see no flower buds or seed follicles, but the foliage revealed small, elliptic to weakly obovate, glabrous leaves that are typical of this species. In this area, excellent populations of *Rhododendon rex* subsp. *rex* with leaves a little larger than typical caught my eye. The road then passed over the boundary into the MDNNR, by a rather forlorn sign at the margins of an old cut-block. We could see healthy high-elevation conifer forest above us, including the sparse crowns of *Larix potaninii* var. *macrocarpa*. We now descended passing somewhat distur-bed and degraded forest, though very diverse, with *Acer*, *Carpinus*, *Lithocarpus*, *Populus*, *Pterocarya* and *Sorbus* being very well represented. From our speeding 4-wheel drive

MABIAN RIVER, DAFENGDING   PETER WHARTON

MATURE 18M TREE OF *MAGNOLIA DAWSONIANA* near Longwo, Meigu – Dafengding National Nature Reserve, s. Sichuan. Notice the dense, horizontal branching of the upper crown   PETER WHARTON

we began to see another magnolia, that our hosts told us was *Magnolia sargentiana*. It was plentiful, often as regenerating coppiced trees close to the road and more excitingly as freestanding trees in intact forests above and below us. Seeing so many specimens in such a rich, protected area brought on feelings of both jubilation and relief in my colleagues and me. The highly ornamental monkey-tailed hornbeam (*Carpinus fangiana*) was scattered amongst more numerous riverside groves of the Chinese walnut (*Juglans cathayensis*), some of these of great size. Furthering our sense of awe was the sight of old growth forests dominated by ancient *Cercidiphyllum*, *Davidia*, *Euptelea*, *Magnolia* and *Tetracentron*. These important archaic genera became more abundant below 2000m and would become for us a botanical signature for the Dafengding region.

We entered the small town of Longwo (meaning: nest of the dragon), beside the Mabian (meaning: remote) in suitably misty, mysterious weather. This logging ghost town was a hub of activity in the 1960s to the 1980s but is now falling back to being an agricultural and herding center. Despite the slightly depressed atmosphere, satellite dishes sprouted from nearly every house, announcing a touch of modernity even here. We stayed at the local guesthouse, which proved clean and comfortable. Our hosts were a delightful couple who provided us with simple, nutritious food throughout our five-day stay. One particular memorable day we traveled a short distance from outside Longwo up the Bamaluojue valley. Here rough pasture was dotted with massive, burnt stumps of *Cercidiphyllum japonicum* var. *sinense.* The scene had certain parallels to the famous pollard oaks, or 'dodders' in Windsor Great Park, UK. Many had also been repeatedly

IMPRESSIVE STEM of *Magnolia dawsoniana,* Meigu – Dafengding National Nature Reserve, s. Sichuan

PETER WHARTON

coppiced and showed a remarkable capacity to regenerate from basal lignotubers or sprouts from residual live bark. Joining these spectral hulks were other coppiced trees including the rare, but here locally numerous, trifoliate maple, *Acer sutchuenense.* However, it was the presence of several coppiced specimens of *Magnolia dawsoniana* that really drew my attention. These grew above a stream on the

sides of heavily grazed benches, amongst a dense mature shrubbery dominated by maples such as *Acer robustum* and *A. oliverianum,* with several species in the *Prunus* Section *Padus.* The magnolias varied from 20cm to nearly 50cm basal diameter – some up to 10m tall – and showed a range of coppicing history. Higher up the surrounding steep hillsides, fine, untouched 20m specimens of *Magnolia dawsoniana,* were mingled with *Acer sterculiaceum* subsp. *franchetii, Carpinus fangiana,* immense *Cercidiphyllum japonicum* var. *sinense, Fraxinus platypoda* and *Tilia chinensis s.l.* These formed the transition into the untouched core of the MDNNR. The few mature trees we could examine at close quarters struck me as typical for the species: strong, often multiple vertical trunks, supporting dense twiggy cumuloid crowns and prolific, horizontally poised spur shoots in the upper branches. *M. dawsoniana* in cultivation often displays such horizontal branch development, no doubt assisted by the considerable and annual weight of massed flowers. The leaves of several specimens from mature to coppiced individuals displayed typical *M. dawsoniana* morphology, uniformly glabrous, though the strong reticulation on the upper leaf surfaces was less strongly developed than those I have seen in cultivation. Two vigorous coppiced individuals I inspected displayed consistently narrowly elliptic leaves. At 7cm long x 5cm wide, these certainly represent the small end of the size spectrum for this species. Koen observed the leaves were also consistently a lighter green than neighbouring specimens of *M. sargentiana.*

At one point I crossed over the stream to examine some enormous *Cercidiphyllum* and became detached from my companions. As I was scrambling back to join them I came across a coppiced trunk of a magnolia with a basal diameter of 1.2m, with foliage very different than any of the coppiced specimens of *M. dawsoniana* I had so far examined. On close examination, the leaves of this tree agreed more with *M. sargentiana;* that is, conspicuously larger leaves, many obovate, generally twice as long as broad and with a large proportion of emarginated leaf apices. These were clearly different compared with the weakly obovate

HUGE SPECIMEN of Cercidiphyllum japonicum var. sinense in the Meigu – Dafengding National Nature Reserve, s. Sichuan   PETER WHARTON

M. dawsoniana and *M. sargentiana* occur together is intriguing. Our travels also took us to several other areas of the Dafengding, where *M. sargentiana* is sporadically distributed. It is conceivable that intermediates occur here and it would not surprise me if subsequent research shows that these two entities are extreme morphological expressions of a complex, where there is active gene flow. Fortunately, we are planning spring visits to this extensive region in the future, so we will be able to make additional determinations based on floral characteristics. We ended our day's work at an old hillside clear-cut, the regenerating scrub above us crushed by a sea of strangulating Chinese gooseberry (*Actinidia* sp.). The old logging road beckoned us higher to the primary forest beyond but that will be for another day.

Our final highlight was a visit to China's southern-most giant panda reserve, the Leibo–Mamize Nature Reserve, located about 60 kilometers south of Longwo It is also a major refuge for *Magnolia sargentiana*. The late Ted Millais mentioned to me that he had visited the

leaves with acuminate tips of the coppiced *M. dawsoniana* specimens. What I found rather puzzling was the generally poor development of any pubescence on the leaf undersides, although some hairs were present on the main and secondary veins. Was this a constant character or had most of the interveinal hairs sloughed off by time we visited this area? Koen noticed the leaves of *M. sargentiana* were commonly colored spinach green. Both of us agreed the inward curving vegetative buds of *M. sargentiana* were a constant distinguishing feature throughout this mixed magnolia population. We also discovered another coppiced specimen and some mature specimens in the forest above. These forest trees had a much more vertical branch orientation in the upper canopy, quite distinct from the *M. dawsoniana* previously described. Unfortunately, time constraints prevented us from making a closer inspection.

From such a cursory examination of these wild populations it would be dangerous to draw final conclusions, yet the possibility that

LEIBO – MAMIZE NATURE RESERVE, s. Sichuan – the southern-most Giant Panda Reserve in China   PETER WHARTON

nearby Shanlenggang area in the fall of 1999, and his inspiring descriptions of this magnolia sparked my curiosity. The reserve covers around 38,000ha of sub-alpine to sub-tropical broad-leaved evergreen forests. Our journey to this reserve started beside the roaring Jinsha River,

SUO LUO MOUNTAIN , Leibo – Mamize Nature Reserve, s. Sichuan. Old stump of *Magnolia sargentiana* with two new stems derived from basal sprouts near the root crown shows the regenerative abilities of this species   PETER WHARTON

where a huge hydroelectric station is being constructed, close to the county town of Leibo. We now passed through spectacular, arid gorges, rustic rural villages alongside rushing torrents, before the road carried us high into the misty remote country of the Xiaoliangshan, a major homeland of the Yi people. Herding of cattle, goats and sheep are important staples of the local economy here. Villages; pasture; forest fragments concentrated along streams; frequent pheasants in the mist. All these are comments in my travel notes as we ascended to 2260m. At high speed on a hairpin bend I caught site of an enormous *Carpinus fangiana* with an impressive domed crown and conspicuous hanging aments (catkins). It was perhaps 25m high, beautifully framed by a water-meadow, while *Cercidiphyllum*, *Davidia*, coppiced *Magnolia sargentiana* and fine stands of *Populus lasiocarpa* abounded on the slopes above. The brand new reserve headquarters is situated in the Yi village of

Gudui at the edge of the reserve. Financial support from the national government and international bodies, such as the World Wildlife Fund has been directed to studying and conserving the giant pandas and other fauna, notably birds, but no botanical investigations have been conducted here of any detail. We were very warmly welcomed by the director, Mr Yang Guji, and his headquarters staff. He proved a most helpful and jocular host.

Several days were spent exploring the densely forested mountain slopes of this reserve above Gudui village. The local Yi people here call *Magnolia sargentiana*, "lipu". The unopened flower buds are of great medicinal value, notably for treating stomach ailments and rheumatism. The impact of flower bud collection on natural seedling regeneration is a concern and will require future study. Ironically, it was easier to enter this forest via an area that was selectively logged in 1956 for its superb *Abies fabri*, which is now regenerating well, I am happy to say. At 2400m on a southwest facing forested slope we found numerous regenerating stumps of Sargent's magnolia, some up to a meter in diameter and coppiced stems up to 7m tall. Smaller trees that had escaped the original logging were growing away well in a matrix of regenerating or intact conifers, *Davidia*, *Lithocarpus* spp., *Tilia chinensis s.l.* and *Tetracentron sinense*. On rocky bluffs or side slopes of old logging roads we recorded a fairly rich rhododendron flora, including *R. argyrophyllum*, *R. calophytum*, *R. ochraceum*, *R. oreodoxa*, *R. pachytrichum*, *R. rex* subsp. *rex* and *R. rubiginosum*. The following day we drove over dirt roads to the alpine meadows that covered one of the major peaks of the reserve, Suo Luo (3300m). On the way up we observed *M. sargentiana* seemed to peter out at 2700m, where the upper sub-alpine forest really started to assert itself. The Xiaoliangshan is an eastern outlier of the typical high elevation subalpine vegetation of the Tibetan Marchlands where so many rhododendrons of the *Lapponica subsection* form extensive moorlands. This mountain has much else to offer the rhododendron enthusiast with *R. decorum* subsp. *cordatum* and *R. huidongense* at high elevations and some stunning groves of *R. rex* subsp. *rex* lower down the mountain are just a sample of the riches here.

Our last days in the Mamize were spent investigating a number of sites on the margins of the main reserve where past logging, especially during the 1950s, and a slash and burn regimen in the 1970s, reduced huge areas in this region to a sea of stumps. Despite further disturbance from grazing and coppicing for fuel over the last ten years, a certain level of forest protection has resulted in tangible forest renewal. Previously coppiced forest trees in a buffer zone around the reserve are now regenerating into multi-stemmed trees. Once you start to recognize the crown color and texture of *M. sargentiana*, whole hillsides of degraded, yet regenerating forest, can be surveyed from a distance. This allows a fairly accurate population survey to be undertaken. On one hillside outside the village of Gudui at 2220m overlooking a grazed valley bottom I managed to pick out nearly a hundred individuals from 3–6m tall. Here, grazing and brushwood collecting has been reduced, though it is still a factor. Professor Tang Ya and his students conducted a further survey in the reserve during April 2007. An estimated total of around 20,000 individuals were recorded, some of great age, and a number were observed up to 30m in height.

We plunged into these regenerating forests to see this forest rebirth. The ability of *M. sargentiana* to regenerate from stumps is quite remarkable and gives us a clue why, despite millennia of terrible destruction, this species still has a bright future when positive conservation measures are undertaken. All the regenerating magnolias grew in association with other tree species, although *Quercus aliena* was particularly abundant. Individual trees ranged from 9–14m tall and were generally multiple-stemmed. Stems measured from 7.5–35cm in diameter. Most stems were drawn upwards as expected in this dense underbrush of bamboo, vines and smaller regenerating trees. Sargent's magnolia prefers free-draining, moist sites, as it was concentrated along moist gullies and moist shady slopes. The magnolia populations we examined in the Mamize were consistent with the morphology of typical *M. sargentiana*, rather than the variance we observed in the Meigu – Dafengding National Nature Reserve.

We came away from our brief trip to this unique spot with a feeling of hope and an appreciation of the conservation measures that had already been implemented here. More

THE XIAOLIANGSHAN forms the northern boundary of the Leibo – Mamize Nature Reserve, s. Sichuan. Timberline *Abies fabri* with understory of *Rhododendron* aff. *huidongense* and *Rhododendron rex* ssp. *rex*   PETER WHARTON

detailed surveys of the Mamize and the whole Dafengding region will undoubtedly reveal other fascinating information on the distribution and status of these magnolias and will help inform the steps required to conserve these species and the forests ecosystems that support them. We are working closely with our Chinese hosts and a number of national and

RHODODENDRON AFF. HUIDONGENSE. Leibo – Mamize Nature Reserve, s. Sichuan. Upper southern slopes of Suo Luo mountain at 3320m

PETER WHARTON

international conservation bodies to ensure our survey work continues and directly assists in protecting more of these rich forest ecosystem 'fragments'. All of us in this program are aware that the needs and cooperation of the local people that live in these regions must always be part of these conservation objectives. Professor Tang Ya is presently working closely with several levels of the Chinese government to coalesce all the national, provincial and county nature reserves in the Dafengding region into one large national park. This protected region would also include some adjacent, presently unprotected forest areas. We wish him well in this endeavour.

ACKNOWLEDGEMENTS
The author wishes to thank Professor Tang Ya (Sichuan University, Chengdu, P.R.C.) and Dr. Koen Camelbeke (Wespelaar Arboretum, Belgium) for reading the manuscript and providing me valuable additional observations and information. I would also like to thank Zhang Liyun (Sichuan University) for providing the location maps used in this article.

Peter Wharton
is Curator of the David C. Lam Asian Garden, University of British Columbia Botanical Garden and Centre for Plant Research

References ■ Cicuzza D, Newton A and Oldfield S (2007), *The Red List of Magnoliaceae,* (Fauna and Flora International, Cambridge, UK) (www.fauna-flora.org, www.globaltrees.org). Treseder NG (1978), *Magnolias,* (Faber and Faber Limited, London, UK) 02–103.

Breeding evergreen azaleas at Glendoick

KENNETH COX

THE EVERGREEN AZALEA BORDER at Glendoick house in late May–early June with *Clematis montana* on the walls

KENNETH COX

THERE IS A CERTAIN DEGREE OF snobbery in rhododendron circles about azaleas, especially evergreen ones. In the USA this became so bad that the azalea people went off and founded their own American Azalea Society as they thought that azaleas were being unfairly ignored. I don't think most people in the UK have any idea of the riches available in the USA and Japan from evergreen or deciduous azaleas. Garden designers putting together plans select the same old Kurume azaleas that Wilson brought over in the early 1900s. They need to wake up, things have moved on and there are far better choices available now. 'Hatsuguri', 'Palestrina', 'Addy Wery'... I would not give any of these garden space these days. Both evergreen and deciduous azaleas are more drought resistant and heat tolerant than most rhododendrons, so for the southeast of England they will probably become more important as drier summers become the norm.

Evergreen or Japanese azaleas are by far the most important part of the rhododendron genus commercially. As houseplants they are produced in millions for the Christmas and early spring markets. Breeders use radiation to encourage mutation and sooner or later they will transplant a yellow gene into a white one to get the elusive yellow evergreen or Japanese azalea. The terms 'evergreen' or 'Japanese' are not really accurate, since many of them are not evergreen and many species come from Taiwan and China. They belong to Section Tsutsusi which is the Japanese word for this group of azaleas and perhaps we should use this term to refer to them. Though not hardy in Scotland, Satsukis, Robin Hills and Encore azaleas (which flower on and off all summer in hot climates) might well be worth trying in southern England as the heat and drought of recent summers should suit them well.

My father, Peter Cox, began hybridising dwarf rhododendrons (the birds such as 'Chikor', 'Ptarmigan' and 'Curlew') in 1959 and in the late 1960s turned his hand to evergreen azaleas. The problem he faced was that most evergreen azaleas he tried in Scotland struggled or died. It was soon apparent that lack of summer heat was

'LEMUR'   KENNETH COX

GLENDOICK® GLACIER　　　　KENNETH COX

winter leaf retention, as well as good flower size and colour.

When I joined in the hybridising game in the early 1980s, I used the first batch of mammals to make further crosses, often using Hachmann azaleas from Germany to augment the available palette. Later on we discovered that Hans Hachmann was in turn using our azaleas to cross with his. Hachmann's 'Drapa' and 'Evita' use 'Squirrel' as one parent. I wanted to create tough hose-in-hose and double-flowered azaleas with good foliage retention in all the colour shades. Glendoick® Dream ['GLE 005'] and Glendoick® Glacier ['GLE 009'] are two examples. For deep red winter foliage, 'Johanna' and 'Marushka' (a Hachmann 'Johanna' hybrid) are hard to beat. I also wanted to get the colour of an American azalea of striking colour – 'Red Red' – which we can't grow, into something suitable for Scotland; we achieved this by crossing it with 'Johanna' to produce Glendoick® Goblin ['GLE 010'], Glendoick® Garnet ['GLE 008'] and Glendoick® Crimson ['GLE 004']. Another challenge was to try to breed whites with good winter leaf retention and large flowers. The key here is to mix the hardiness of the deciduous white *R. kiusianum* with the evergreen 'Mucronatum' and then grow on several generations. 'Panda' is excellent but semi-deciduous. 'Panda' x 'Mucronatum' gave us the huge flowered 'Arctic Fox' but it was not as hardy as we wanted. We crossed this back onto

the main cause of death; wood did not ripen sufficiently to survive the winters and so plants tended to take 2 steps forward and then 2 steps back, losing most of their growth over winter. He tried Kurume, Satsuki, Glenn Dale and many others, but most survived only a short time. The few good ones such as *Rhododendron kiusianum* and its hybrids such as 'Kermesina' and 'Diamant' were small-flowered and not very evergreen but they were tough and reliable. He was sure it would be possible to combine the large flowers of the tender azaleas with the toughness of the small flowered ones.

Using *R. kiusianum* and some new forms of *R. nakaharae* from Polly Hill and others, he began making crosses. He had immediate success with his first few crosses, and 'Panda' (using the tender large flowered 'Everest' as the other parent) is now probably the best selling white azalea in the UK with 'Squirrel' one of the best known reds. The bird names were running out, so my father switched to mammals which provide appealing names such as 'Beaver', 'Wombat', 'Lemur' etc. These azaleas were selected on the basis of toughness, reliability, compactness and good

'KOROMO SHIKIBU' white and purple forms

KENNETH COX

GLENDOICK® SNOWFLAKES   KENNETH COX

the Satsukis are hardy for us. Perhaps we will use Glenn Dales and Robin Hills as a bridge. We have now also started breeding deciduous azaleas, too. Watch this space.

If you fancy doing some rhododendron breeding but are short of space or patience, then evergreen azaleas are a great choice. They flower very young, are easy to root and take up so little room. You can easily grow them in pots till they flower, give away the poorer ones, most of which will be perfectly acceptable garden plants. But don't take the easy option of crossing common azaleas with one another – you'll just get more of the same. Try to breed something new or different: early flowering, late flowering, good foliage, more intense orange... and so on.

Petal blight, little recognised, but now all over the UK and Europe, is the scourge of evergreen azaleas. It tends to strike in late May and early June, turning the flowers to mush, sometimes before they have even opened, particularly in warm and wet weather. You can spray *myclobutanil* (Systhane) on the opening buds to halt it.

'Diamant White' and from this we selected Glendoick® Snowflakes ['GLE 001']. This was previously known as 'Rescued White' before we named it officially. The origin of this name is that when I tried to move the original plant, it broke off at the root. In order to save it, I made the whole plant into cuttings. Thankfully they rooted well. You may also wonder about the names and codes on those varieties with 'Glendoick' in the name. As Glendoick® is a registered trademark, the name is a trade designation and the code is the registered name. This gives us a degree of protection as other nurseries may not sell them without permission and is a cheaper alternative to patenting.

Currently, we are trialling strap-petalled azaleas. These are selections made in Japan of several species where the petals are very narrow, giving a spidery effect. The best are 'Koromo Shikibu' and its white form. They are not all that hardy and tend to be semi-deciduous but they have great potential if we can cross them into hardier more evergreen varieties. A future project is to get some Satsuki blood into our hardy azaleas to see if there is any potential for introducing multi-colours. These ancient Japanese azaleas are late flowering and popular for bonsai. They have bicolour and multi-coloured flowers, often with flecks and spotting and sometimes with several colours on one plant. At the moment, none of

GLENDOICK® ROSEBUD   KENNETH COX

EVERGREEN AZALEA PRODUCTION AT GLENDOICK

KENNETH COX

CLIMATE NOTE

Glendoick is on the east coast of Scotland, a few miles from the Tay estuary. The coldest winters recorded have reached –18°C but this happens only a few times a century. A cold winter is usually more like –12°C. Summers have few summer days over 27°C. Rainfall is 600–760mm annually. Our greatest problem is late spring frosts after periods of mild weather: flowers and growth are often frosted and bark-split can result.

THE GLENDOICK EVERGREEN AZALEAS

'Arctic Fox' ('Panda' x 'Mucronatum') – Large pure white flowers. Furry pale green leaves. The least hardy of the Glendoick whites but with the largest flowers.

'Beaver' (*R. nakaharae* x) – Compact, dark red, late June. Grown by Braevallich nurseries.

'Chinchilla' ('Chippewa' x 'Vida Brown') Hose-in-hose light red flowers. Grown by Braevallich nurseries.

'Chipmunk' ('Chippewa' x 'Vida Brown') Hose-in-hose bright pink flowers, very compact.

Glendoick® Crimson ['GLE04'] ('Squirrel' x 'Red Red') Very dark red flowers in May. Excellent foliage but a bit straggly.

Glendoick® Dream ['GLE005'] ('Panda' x 'Rokoko') Double, ruffled purplish-red flowers in May. Dark green leaves, bronze in winter. Very compact.

Glendoick® Ermine ['GLE006'] ('Panda' x 'Mucronatum') Large pure white flowers.

Glendoick® Garnet ['GLE008'] ('Squirrel' x 'Red Red') 'Hot' deep red flowers May.

Glendoick® Glacier ['GLE009'] ('Panda' x 'Rokoko') Double white flowers.

Glendoick® Goblin ['GLE010'] ('Squirrel' x 'Red Red') Hot red flowers, petaloid stamens. Excellent deep green shiny leaves, reddish in winter.

Glendoick® Rosebud ['GLE022'] ('Eisprinzessin' x 94/3A) Double pale pink in early May.

Glendoick® Snowflakes ['GLE001'] ('Arctic Fox' x 'Diamant White') Pure white in late May, good foliage retention.

'Lemur' (*R. nakaharae* x 'Vuyk's Scarlet') Deep pink, low growing, late May.

'Marmot' ('Vida Brown' x 'Vuyk's Scarlet') Deep purplish pink.

'Opossum' ('Purpurtraum' x 'Blue Danube') Rich purple, spreading, compact, evergreen.

'Panda' ('Everest' x *R. kiusianum* 'White') Pure white with some yellow spotting. Long our best seller.

'Pine Marten' ('Eisprinzessin' x 94/3A) Large-flowered single pink, May.

'Racoon' (*R. nakaharae* x) Bright red flowers in June–July, compact, spreading.

'Red Panda' ('Squirrel' x 'Red Red') masses of bright red flowers, very compact.

'Squirrel' (*R. nakaharae* x 'Galathea') Small bright scarlet flowers in June.

'Stoat' ('Kermesina' x 'Lemur') Bright pink. (No longer grown.)

'Wombat' (*R. nakaharae* 'Mariko' x 'Gaiety') Pink in early June, spreading ground cover.

Kenneth Cox

is the author of many books on rhododendrons including the definitive colour guide to rhododendron and azalea species, The Encyclopedia of Rhododendron Species, co-authored with his father, Peter. His most recent book, Rhododendrons and Azaleas, A Colour Guide, covers both evergreen and deciduous azaleas in detail.

www.glendoick.com

RHS Garden Rosemoor

On the A3124, Great Torrington, Devon, EX38 8PH

National RHS Rhododendron Show

Saturday 26 & Sunday 27 April, 10am - 5pm

60 classes covering all types of Rhododendrons
Includes Camellia and Magnolia show

Admission: Normal Garden Entry

Tel: 01805 624067
Email: rosemooradmin@rhs.org.uk
www.rhs.org.uk/rosemoor

Registered Charity No. 222879/SCO38262

Royal
Horticultural
Society

Arduaine Garden, Argyll: An historical perspective

The evolution of a magical rhododendron garden on Scotland's West Coast

JOHN M HAMMOND

LOOKING NORTH across Asknish Bay provides a clear perspective of the wooded peninsula and the white structure of Arduaine House, now the Loch Melfort Hotel

JOHN HAMMOND

SET AMID THE RUGGED mountains, moors and lochs on Scotland's West Coast is the fishing port of Oban, gateway to the Western Isles. No one can fail to be impressed by the scenic grandeur of Argyll's wild, rocky coastline with its myriad of isles, lochs and peninsulas that make it a photogenic destination when the snow still lingers on the mountains in early May. South out of Oban the A816 twists and turns for 40 miles as it weaves a path through the rocky strata towards Lochgilphead. Around the halfway mark the Arduaine peninsula juts out on the west side of the A816, pointing towards the islands of the Inner Hebrides that are scattered on the horizon, of which the largest are Shuna, Luing, Lunga and the Garvellachs; beyond them there is nothing but the Atlantic until the Labrador Coast is reached.

At 56°13'N and 5°34'W the peninsula is similar in latitude to Labrador City, in northern Canada, which speaks volumes as to the influence of the North Atlantic Drift on Scotland's West Coast.

Immediately to the east of Arduaine is the 841ft summit of Beinn Chaorach, an ideal location from which to get a better perspective of the vast expanse of coastline. The peninsula itself rises to the 239ft summit of An Cnap, the site of an Iron Age Dun (fortification), but in reality the promontory and its woodlands are lost in the immensity of the landscape, the sea and the sky; a reminder that, with this scenic grandeur as a backdrop, many West Coast gardens had no need for the services of a formal landscape designer such as Capability Brown. Beyond the white walls of Arduaine House, built by J Arthur Campbell and in later years better known as the Loch Melfort Hotel, the pathway flanked with daffodils leads down a slope beneath the overhanging boughs of a row of flowering cherry trees, which together form a spectacular entrance to the garden each spring. The garden itself sits in the protective curve of the southern slope of the peninsula, which affords some shelter from the northeast and northwest winds; the rainfall being relatively heavy at an average of 60 inches per year until the mid-1980s, and closer to 75 inches since that date.[7, 15]

THE ORIGINS OF ARDUAINE

James Arthur Campbell (1850–1929), who preferred to be known as 'Arthur', was a member of the House of Inverawe, one of the oldest branches of Clan Campbell and the fourth son of six children. He spent his youth on the

Auchendarroch Estate, at Lochgilphead, where his father, Alexander Campbell, 1st of Auchendarroch (Gaelic for 'field of the oak'), had planted numerous exotic trees and shrubs in the temperate climate. William J Hooker, Professor of Botany at the University of Glasgow and later Director of Kew Gardens, is credited with laying out the grounds of Kilmory Castle in 1830, another Campbell estate a short distance to the east of Lochgilphead.[2] Hooker furnished many of the exotic shrubs and plants that flourished at Kilmory. Around 1830 there were very few sources in Scotland for exotic plant material and, as the development of the woodland gardens at Auchendarroch, later known as the Oakfield Estate, fits into this timeframe it is more than likely that Hooker was involved to some extent with the contents of this garden.[3] These plantings probably aroused J Arthur Campbell's early interest in horticulture, to which he was eventually to devote a great deal of his life. His eldest brother, Archibald J Campbell, was expected to become the 15th of Inverawe and 2nd of Auchendarroch; so, in common with many other Campbell sons over the centuries, J Arthur Campbell had to pursue a career and living elsewhere. It would appear that Arthur spent several years in Ceylon and India, and his descendants suspect he worked on tea plantations in Assam for a time. It would seem obvious that with his interests in shrubs and trees he must have visited the Himalayas at some point as Assam is near to the mountains. He returned to Scotland in 1885/86 to see his aged father and met Ethel Margaret Bruce whom he married in 1887. Arthur accepted the offer of a job with Ethel's father, John Bruce, who owned a firm of corn merchants in Edinburgh and he remained with the firm until John Bruce died in 1895, when Ethel inherited her share of his fortune.[1]

It was only natural that on retirement J Arthur Campbell should wish to return to his native Argyll and pursue his interest in shrubs and trees, so he decided to search for a property that had potential for development as a woodland garden. But the rugged, rocky coastline with its small isles and inlets was particularly difficult to access from the mainland; so, as Sir Ilay Campbell explains, the family tradition has it that in 1898 Arthur hit on a novel method of finding a home:[4]

He therefore decided to search for a property which had potential scope for the development of a woodland garden, and to this end he and his wife spent the summer cruising in a yacht exploring the many lochs, sounds and islands which form the coastline of Argyll. Whenever they spied a likely spot, they would make enquiries as to land available to purchase.

Eventually they arrived in Loch Melfort, certainly one of the most beautiful of all, and here their search was destined to end. They saw a green peninsula jutting out into the loch backed by an almost complete semi-circle of comparatively low hills giving shelter from the north and east. The estate, then known as Asknish, chanced to be for sale ...

In the opening paragraph of Arthur's journal begun in 1903, in which he recorded the planting operations on the Arduaine Estate, he wrote:[6]

In May 1897 I purchased three farms, Asknish, Kilbride and Barnlannich, from Colonel McIver Campbell Lochgair. As a part of the bargain was that I was not to call myself 'Campbell of Asknish', I called the Estate 'Arduaine', ie (Gaelic for) the 'Green Point', from the greeness [sic] of the point on 'Asknish Farm' on which Arduaine House is built.

In reality it was Ethel's fortune that enabled them to purchase the three farms, build a home and develop the gardens.[1] Whilst the area is generally referred to as Loch Melfort, from the name of the sea-loch that runs inland in a northeasterly direction, Arduaine House and Garden actually look out over Asknish Bay, at the northern end of the Sound of Jura. It is worth noting that at the time Arthur purchased Asknish Farm the 1000 yard peninsula was almost completely bare, windswept, poor farming pasture, apart from *"7 ash trees at back of garden ... about a dozen stunted oaks on the hills near the garden"*, the remaining trees that made up a total of 92 were located close to the main road:[6]

I wished to commence operations for laying out a Garden and building in the summer of 1897 but the farm Tennant [sic] Mr MacKechnie would not allow me to do anything until his lease was up on the 28th

May 1898. In the summer of 1898 Mrs Campbell and I came here in our yacht Calisaya and lay in Asknish Bay for some days – we then fixed definitely the sites for the House, Stables and Garden ... I then moved up from Kilbride [one of the three farms purchased from the McIvers] *a two roomed wooden building which I had erected there the previous year for a Keeper and put this up in one corner of the gardens as a tool shed and put a stove in it and used one room as a "bothy" for a man to live in. Simpson* [his father's gardener at Auchendarroch] *and the man then fenced in the ground laid off for the Garden with a wire fence and rabbit netting and then commenced to lay out this garden.*

A note in the margin records *"1st sod of the Garden was turned in August 1898."* Arthur's comments relate to the establishment of a kitchen garden to supply *"Arduaine Mansion House"* on which building work commenced in September of the same year. Work on the structure of the house got off to a bad start as the contractor's work was shoddy, so the partly completed structure had to be demolished and rebuilt. It would be 1905 before the construction of the two-storey house with its gabled dormers was completed. One wonders if the initial attempts to create a kitchen garden fared any better, as there are numerous references to the ravages of the rabbits, so in 1902 this area was enclosed by a stout wooden fence. The timber-framed Arduaine Cottage, built in 1903 in the garden to accommodate the Head Gardener, was probably lived in by Arthur and Ethel until the House was completed.

Arthur was clearly a 'man on a mission' as the planting of shelter for Lower Garden, the area running from the Inside Garden down to the sea, had commenced in the autumn of 1898 when the Glen was fenced and planted with Douglas firs. These were quickly decimated by the rabbits to whom the fence was not a barrier given their burrowing capabilities! The Lower Garden was envisaged as a semi-formal garden with shrub borders and a pond, however, an extensive part of this area was originally bog-land. Oral tradition has it that shortly after the property was purchased a start was made on developing an area of semi-formal gardens close to the House, however, this project had to be abandoned because of the predominantly southwesterly winds which, laden with salt-water, funnelled-up the neck of the promontory and damaged the young plants. The planting of a shelter-belt in this area would have entirely spoilt the dramatic views from the front of the House, so the semi-formal garden was laid-out some distance away. Arthur continued his experimentation with shelter-belt planting at least up to 1907 and the plantings were ultimately mainly of European larch; the first bamboos being planted in 1903.

The Campbells were friendly with that exceptional Highland gentleman of outstanding foresight, Osgood Mackenzie. Dignified by a massive flowing beard, he was a highly regarded naturalist, a man of many skills and a very great gardener. There are many similarities between the estate and garden that Osgood created at Inverewe and that which Arthur was seeking to establish at Arduaine. Looking at a photograph of Inverewe, taken from across Loch Ewe in 1900, it is clear that the gardens at both places are located on the south side of a promontory, the house was built at the neck of the peninsula, the upper levels of the headland were still bare moorland whilst the lower elevations were covered with areas of shelter-belt plantings that Arthur needed to replicate. Wooden fencing was used in an effort to control the numerous rabbits and deer whilst stone was used to surround the Walled Garden. One can conjecture that the small yacht *Calisaya* was a regular visitor to Loch Ewe, where there was anchorage for yachts close to the house, as the Campbells would have had an able mentor in Osgood Mackenzie.

There is little doubt that Arthur sourced plant material from Auchendarroch where his father's extensive woodland gardens contained many plants, specimen trees and a large, sheltered walled garden. Arthur is also said to have financially supported various expeditions to the Himalayas, although no records have been found to date.[7] Planting in the woodland garden had commenced by 1922 when George Watt, the Campbell's last chauffeur, started work at Arduaine and the first rhododendrons were planted in 'The Glen'. These first plantings included *R. arboreum* subsp. *zeylanicum*, raised from wild seed collected on the central plateau of Ceylon, and the plants sent to Scotland in a tea chest. Six wonderful specimens have survived and are said to be the best in cultivation. During the 1920s there was a team of six gardeners working on the estate including the Irishman John Brennan, who appears to have been the head gardener.[8] George Watt remembers the *Eucalyptus urnigera* being planted in the early-1930s.

Through the many 'connections' of the wider Campbell Family, Arthur was able to source and exchange plant material with many of the illustrious Scottish rhododendron enthusiasts in the years after the First World War, thus by the late 1920s there were some 220 varieties of rhododendrons growing at Arduaine, of which the majority were species.[6] Notable amongst these are three plants of *R. griffithianum* that have thrived to become very large specimens, *R. arboreum* subsp. *nilagiricum* from the Indian peninsula (a close relative of *R. arboreum* subsp. *zeylanicum*), the August flowering *R. auriculatum* that forty years ago had reached 30ft in height and 35ft in girth and amongst the large-leaved specimens, a superb *R. giganteum* – the first of its species to flower in Britain.

Besides Osgood Mackenzie at Inverewe, and later Sir George Campbell at Crarae (Sir Ilay's father), Arthur knew Col FRS Balfour of Dawyck whose glen garden arboretum was later to become an outstation of the RBG, Edinburgh.[1]

Whilst most references credit Arthur with the original development of the garden it is clear from various documents that the ladies of Arduaine House had a significant impact on the layout, plantings and maintenance of the garden. This is to some extent evident in the words of Arthur when he described how in 1898 he and his wife had *"fixed definitely the sites for the House, Stables and Garden."* Sometime later, probably around 1910, instructions on the setting-out of the paths and beds in the lower part of the garden were apparently issued

by Mrs Campbell from the top of the knoll outside the garden gate. Mrs Ethel M Campbell became a member of The Rhododendron Association shortly after its formation in 1927, probably around the same time as Sir George Campbell of Crarae Lodge.

Osgood Mackenzie passed away in 1922 and Arthur was deeply affected by the loss of his mentor. Following James Arthur Campbell's

THE CLIFF PATH also provides some superb views across the Inside Garden and out across Asknish Bay   JOHN HAMMOND

own death in 1929 the Arduaine estate passed to his son Bruce, although his mother continued to live at Arduaine House.

THE GRADUAL DECLINE OF ARDUAINE GARDEN

Brigadier Bruce Atta Campbell spent most of his life in active service up until the time his mother died in 1936. In the immediate aftermath of J Arthur Campbell's death in 1929, and with Bruce away in the Services, there appears to have been a lack of leadership and little sense of direction so far as Arduaine Garden was concerned; certainly any further development of the garden seems to have been put on hold

THIS VIEW across the garden towards the Cliff Path demonstrates many of the attractive features that make Arduaine a magical woodland garden

JOHN HAMMOND

Yuille came to Arduaine to look after Iain and his sister Jean when they and the garden were in their infancy. She stayed on after the nursery days to give her full-time attention and expertise to the garden. Unfortunately, the onset of WWII had a major impact on the garden. Bruce commanded the 8th Argyll and Sutherland Highlanders, becoming their Hon Colonel from 1940 to 1953; Margaret was involved in voluntary work, Jean left home to serve with the Royal Navy and whilst Nanny Yuille valiantly struggled on in the garden, she was unable

indefinitely. John Brennan, Arthur's head gardener, who didn't get along with Bruce, decided in 1929 to seek pastures new at the site of a new house and garden under construction at Arisaig.[8, 9] After the death of his mother in 1936, Bruce and his wife Margaret moved to Arduaine House, some of the gardening staff were retained and the gardens are said to have been well maintained up to the outbreak of hostilities in WWII, but no further development work took place. During this period Bruce and his wife were spending a considerable period away from home as a result of Bruce's career in the Armed Services and Margaret's voluntary work that in time led to her being Head of the Red Cross in Scotland. Despite these major distractions, they both took an interest in the garden as and when time permitted. Given Bruce's disability from a heart problem and his wounding at Gallipoli in WWI is not surprising that his capacity for work in the garden was limited.[1] They corresponded with several horticultural friends and botanical institutions, and Margaret Campbell in the 1930s became a member of The Rhododendron Association, probably taking over the membership of Bruce's mother, Ethel.

Their daughter Jean took over responsibility for the maintenance of the garden, aided by Miss Yuille, the former family nanny. Nanny

to cope on her own. Jimmy Ferguson, the estate odd job man, was the only person who was expected to work in the garden during the war years, but since he had to do everything else as well it is probable that the garden will have seen little of him.[3] Given the high rainfall, together with the high rate of growth in the temperate climate, the woodland area quickly grew too dense, choking-out the plants beneath it, and much of this area of the garden became wild. During the war, and afterwards, a series of severe gales caused chaos in various areas of the garden and many plants were damaged by falling trees. The loss of trees caused gaps in the shelter-belt and allowed the wind and salt spray to penetrate the woodland areas.

In the post-war years the Estate could not afford the cost of gardeners, but in any case in the economic climate there were no able-bodied staff available and it would have been extremely difficult to get gardeners to move to this remote location. The return of Jean from war service provided another pair of helping hands but the task was too large for her and Nanny Yuille. In 1946 Margaret Campbell became a member of the newly-formed RHS Rhododendron Group. Iain Campbell, the eldest son of Bruce and Margaret, and his wife Colena were both experts in the field of horticulture and lived away from

Arduaine. Grace Margaret Campbell, CBE was a distinguished nurse in Brisbane, Australia and was Matron-in-Chief in service overseas at the outbreak of WWII. In 1948 Bruce received a knighthood in recognition of his years of service and the following year became Lord Lieutenant of Argyll. Brigadier Sir Bruce Campbell died in August 1954, his wife passed away on 12th January 1957 and the estate passed to his son Iain, who with his wife Colena took on the maintenance of the garden.

A number of previous reports have suggested that the Campbell Family had little interest in caring for and maintaining the garden after Arthur Campbell passed away. Discussions over the years with members of the family indicate this view is completely erroneous, and there is a world of difference between the work needed to upkeep the garden as it was when Arthur died, and the labour involved in continuing to open up the woodland areas and develop the garden. It is often forgotten that many such gardens as Arduaine were essentially family gardens and the other 'branches' of the family would also help at times to look after the garden, as Gillie Mackie Campbell, of the 'Stonefield' Campbells, recalls:[10]

THE LONG BORDER has changed considerably over the years, however, there has been a greenhouse in this location since the 1930s   JOHN HAMMOND

Iain and Colena Campbell came back (after WWII) to Arduaine about 1947 or so. My husband (Lorne) and Colena were brother and sister and Colena and I had been friends for years over our shared enjoyment of Highland Ponies. During the late-fifties and early-sixties, when the National Trust Meteor was on her West Highland cruises (each May), Colena and I 'inspired' all available family and friends to give the garden a tidy before the cruise came. Also living at Arduaine were Iain's sister Jean (an ex-market gardener), Nanny Yuille who had been Iain and Jean's Nanny, Mr. Watt the chauffeur, handyman and gardener, and the nanny to the youngest Campbells, Iain and Colena's Nigel and Sheila, Nanny Bonner. We all used to set to and make the garden tidy.

By this time the garden was becoming increasingly mature, the trees having grown up with the shrubs they were protecting, and the intended selective thinning not having taken place meant that both the trees and plants were being drawn-up towards the light, resulting in them being thin and spindly instead of the natural spreading growth. Of necessity, Major Iain and Colena Campbell's many activities left them less time to take up the challenge that the garden represented in those years. Major Iain was heavily involved with the affairs of Scottish Agriculture and it fell to Colena, Jean Campbell and Miss Yuille to persevere with the garden. They continued to have some voluntary help from George Watt, Sir Bruce's chauffeur, and Mr Bates, Major Iain's houseman.

Major Iain and Colena entered trusses in the early Scottish Rhodo-dendron Shows, inaugurated by the NTS in 1953 and held in the McLellan Galleries in Glasgow's teeming Sauchiehall Street. Comp-etition was fierce amongst the highly regarded gardens on Scotland's West Coast, nevertheless, Arduaine gained many awards up to the early 1960s. Colena was also responsible for the inspired planting in the 1960s of the row of cherry trees (*Prunus* 'Kanzan', 'Tai Haku' and 'Ukon') along the pathway that links the garden to the House.[15]

In 1960 the decision was taken by the Stonefield Campbells to sell Stonefield Castle, the estate being divided into two lots, the House and Gardens being sold as a hotel, and the southern policies being sold to the Forestry Commission. Some years ago Gillie Mackie Campbell, of the Stonefield Campbells, and the author discussed the origin of the heron statue in the Lower Pond at Arduaine. It appears that the Campbell Family removed a number of items prior to the sale of Stonefield Castle Estate; as Gillie explains:[10]

THE ORNAMENTAL heron has seen many changes in the past fifty years whilst guarding its namesake pond

JOHN HAMMOND

It is quite odd about the heron in the Lower Pond (at Arduaine), as neither Nigel or Sheila knew that it had come from Stonefield and Colena only told me about the time she left Arduaine... Apparently, she and Iain had gone down one night and "abstracted" it from the South Lodge pond!

When Mr. Davidian (RBGE) was staying with us (at Stonefield House) and trying to impart some rhododendron knowledge into our heads, I remember going up to Arduaine and being astonished by the Magnolia campbellii. *Mr. Davidian really got Lorne and I enthused.*

With the passing years, and the advancing age of these hard-working volunteers, it became necessary to consider the future of the garden, so in 1964 it was reluctantly decided to split up the Arduaine Estate into lots for sale. Arduaine House was cleared ready for separate sale and, during the clearance work, all the estate and garden records were burnt except those family records that are retained by the Inverawe Campbell Family. Arduaine House was sold in 1964 and became the Loch Melfort Motor Inn, later renamed the Loch Melfort Hotel. Around the same time clearance work also took place in the garden itself as it was hoped that someone with the resources to fully restore and look after the garden would purchase it. Sir Ilay Campbell recalled in 1966:[4]

In the last few years, however, large-scale rescue operations have taken place; clearing and judicious removal of some of the overgrown plants has given space for the development of those remaining. Careful thinning has provided room for new plantings, and it is now possible to see these really inspiring shrubs to their full advantage.

When Major Iain sold Arduaine House in 1964 maintenance of the garden seems to have ceased completely. Nanny Yuille retired to her own little house in Benderloch, Argyll and she was very upset about the state of the garden and its future. Nanny Yuille is fondly remembered by all the family; Gillie Mackie Campbell has written:[10]

I think a tiny part of Arduaine Garden, close under the entrance block, is still called 'Nanny Yuille's Garden'. She was tiny and bent double and she loved all the tiny plants – they were on the same level!

Prior to retirement Nanny Yuille continued to labour for long days in the garden, often after twilight had passed, when one of the family would notice she was missing and someone would be deputised to go and look for Nanny Yuille with a torch! It is very appropriate that when she passed away it was arranged for her ashes to be scattered in the garden. Some means of recognising Nanny Yuille's many years of caring for Arduaine, often single-handed through

WWII and the difficult times that followed the cessation of hostilities, is long overdue.

Little interest was shown in the purchase and restoration of the garden, so hope that a new owner could be found was gradually fading and some other use for the property seemed inevitable. Nothing had been decided when, on the night of January 14th, 1968 a stiff south-westerly wind that had been blowing all evening reached hurricane force around midnight along Scotland's West Coast. During the storm, which lasted until 4.00am, the anemometer at the Royal Navy base at Faslane, on the Gareloch, was blown down, registering a wind speed of 118mph; and there were suggestions that the severity of the hurricane may well have been greater at the more exposed locations along the Coast. It was not until daylight that the devastation at Arduaine became apparent; the hurricane had felled a large number of the taller trees, the woodland area being the worst affected, and these were strewn around all over the place, as if in protest at the incomprehensible power and capacity of Nature for destruction. Some trees were supported by others, others leaned dangerously on their neighbours. Many of the trees covered the under-plantings and there were large areas of the garden that were inaccessible. Only seven years earlier the Campbell Family had cleared the fallen trees and debris from the main areas of the garden, and perhaps it was not surprising in the aftermath of the hurricane that the Campbell Family decided it was no longer viable to sell the property as a garden and it was thought the land might eventually become part of a holiday home development scheme.[7]

In the late winter of 1971 the property was advertised for sale through the Edinburgh office of John D Wood, the well-known International Estate Agents, the property particulars indicated that the agents had obtained a verbal understanding from Argyll County Council that an application for planning permission, i.e., building developments of some kind, would be allowed within the confines of the existing garden.[8]

THE RESTORATION OF ARDUAINE GARDEN

By 1971 seven years had passed since the garden had received any maintenance, a longer period than the duration of WWII whose adverse effect on gardens is well documented. In 1971 Edmund AT and Harry C Wright were engaged in the creation of a garden at Duror, to the north of the village of Appin, some 27 miles north of Oban. The Wright Brothers were retired nurserymen from Cranham, near Upminster, Essex, where they owned and managed the Royal Oak Nurseries which sold a wide range of shrubs and trees, including rhododendrons, azaleas and camellias.[11]

These two horticulturists were intrigued by the challenge of having the opportunity to rescue and restore Arduaine Garden, having visited the property only days before the closing date for offers. Edmund and Harry were concerned as to what might have happened to the garden if the unique site had fallen into the hands of a property developer, however, what they required to make the purchase viable was a supply of clear water for both domestic and irrigation purposes. So, the discovery of two clear water springs in the garden was instrumental in the decision to raise their offer on the morning of the final day for offers to be considered. Thus the deal was clinched; it had been a very close-run thing that a lifeline became available for rescuing the garden, and Edmund (Ed) Wright explained their thoughts and activities in the immediate aftermath of acquiring the garden:[8]

We took over the garden on November 11th, 1971 and in the remaining weeks up to Christmas our activities centred round the old timber cottage [Arduaine Cottage] dating from 1903. It was necessary to make it reasonably habitable, it having been unoccupied since 1943, or thereabouts, according to George Watt. George was to prove a mine of information having started work with Arthur Campbell in the early twenties. We spent Christmas in Essex with our family, and whilst there took the opportunity to buy many of the tools we were going to need on our return to Argyll in the New Year.

On arriving back we immediately set to work, our main task being to open up paths long overwhelmed by nature and so the smoke from bonfires hung over the garden for the remainder of the winter and became a familiar sight to a neighbour who lived on the Isle of Luing. In the spring she came to see us and said her visit was prompted by the clouds of smoke that she had seen rising from the garden during the winter . . .

The Wright Brothers had no illusions that years of work lay ahead of them, not only in terms of clearing the storm damage, scattered debris, undergrowth, saplings, and the removal of plants and trees that were dead or in poor condition; but also in regard to developing the garden from the wider foundations that had been laid by Arthur Campbell. In the years following Arthur's death in 1929 virtually no new areas had been planted and much of the woodland area remained to be opened up and developed as a garden. Accordingly, the work needed to be planned and taken forward a stage at a time and in the winter of 1978 Ed Wright reviewed the progress that Harry and himself had made in the Inside Garden, the Lower garden and in the woodland area over the past seven years:[12]

Visitors enter the garden on its eastern boundary ... At a slightly lower level on the left is a small lawn. A newly constructed flight of steps and gravel path lead off through beds of rhododendrons and shrubs towards the sea. Much alteration has been made here in the last six months; gone is the tangle of Pernettya and heathers, previously a haven for rabbits. Several plants have been re-sited ... quite a number of additional young plants can be seen, mainly species, and all recently planted.

A little further on and we begin to see the start of our major alterations. Gone is the fence that enclosed the vegetable garden, the old fruit trees and the bushes have been taken out and the paths and plots grassed over. Now one looks across a large lawn to a mixed bank of trees and shrubs. There are many diversions possible but we shall continue along the present path. The small glasshouse contains a number of tender rhododendrons, all very small and in due course destined for planting outside. The old yew hedge which grew on the seaward side of the path has been removed and the whole area is much improved. We now approach a junction in the path, on the left is the start of the Water Garden ... we can now continue straight on in to what was then a wilderness ... The path now turns left on to the garden road [later The Glen]. To the north it is bounded by a steep rocky bank,

with the 'Wood' above that. This bank has now been cleared of the existing trees and undergrowth, a retaining wall has been built alongside the road, and planting of the bank has begun. It is, however, extremely dry and things will be difficult to establish. Across the road is a newly constructed sunken path. This was excavated to take in one of the old drainage ditches which was not particularly attractive, after having been cleared of the tangle that grew there. The area is now planted with dwarf rhododendrons, primulas and hostas and in a year or two this will be a great improvement. We are now approaching the start of the woodland.

I will give a brief description of the state in which we found (the woodland), and of the work that has been done over the past seven years. It is doubtful if much thinning had ever been attempted. The trees are predominantly larch, with a few Acer, cherry, Pinus, Abies, birch and the odd Ulmus and Tilia. The majority have grown tall and thin and are between ninety and a hundred feet high. Under this dense canopy were planted many fine rhododendrons, and of course they have suffered badly from the lack of light. Indeed, many of them have never flowered, while others produced only a few blossoms yearly. The first winter was spent clearing the floor of the 'Wood', and opening up paths that had been choked for years. The second winter saw us felling a few trees here and there and continuing the removal of undergrowth and rubbish. During this time we visited several other local gardens, and noted how essential good light was to the growing of rhododendrons in the west of Scotland. Drastic action was called for if we were ever going to see some of our best plants in full flower, but felling trees in a wood full of rhododendrons is not an easy task, particularly when the trees are some ninety feet or more high. In the last five years the trees have been carefully thinned and the light has flooded in ... Needless to say, we are still felling trees and this spring will see several of our old rhododendrons in flower for the first time.

Ed Wright's understatement of "felling a few trees here and there" cannot begin to convey the enormity of the physical work undertaken by the Wright Brothers to transform the garden. After clearing away the dozens of trees strewn around by the 1968 hurricane, Ed and Harry felled hundreds of huge conifers, which needed to be sawn-up and carried away; then vast amounts of brambles and shrubbery were carefully cut away without disturbing the established plant collections lying beneath. In the midst of this the Wright Brothers retained ownership of their Royal Oak nurseries for many years, which was a distraction that necessitated regular visits to Essex.

LOOKING TO THE FUTURE

By the early 1990s two decades of continual heavy work in the garden, often from dawn to dusk seven days a week, had more than begun to take their toll on Ed and Harry Wright and they began to consider their options as to the arrangements under which the future of the garden could be assured. Reminiscing in 1996, about the years they had spent restoring the garden since the purchase of the garden in 1971, Ed wrote:[8]

During the next 21 years the work continued (it may sound a long time) and the seasons came and went with what seemed increasing speed, a recognised reality as one gets older, but the work continued. Vast quantities of undergrowth had to be removed and the roots grubbed out, bonfires seldom went out during the winter months. The woodland was scoured for rock with which to build retaining walls and when we ran out within our own boundaries we brought it in from the beach or off the hill behind the garden. Equally large amounts of gravel and stones for making new paths came in from the beach, indeed we cleared the beach of such material and had to wait for the annual scouring effect of the winter storms to renew the deposits.

New lawns were levelled, often necessitating the removal of thick mats of montbretia which had naturalised and become almost as bad as the common bluebell, of which there are millions. Old drainage ditches were piped and filled in with gravel from the beach.

The existing ponds were tiny, the round pond in the grove being more in keeping with a suburban garden, they were all enlarged. The pond now referred to as the Heron Pond was about a third its present size and

surrounded by bushes that made it seem even smaller. It was excavated by hand to its present size and the other ponds at a higher level are all new and excavated from a wilderness of undergrowth and rubbish that had been dumped in a boggy area over many years. Paths in the vicinity of the ponds were virtually non-existent – likewise the area paved with stone which was laid after the ponds had been extended.

THIS PART OF THE GARDEN was created by the Wright Brothers from an area of boggy land and demonstrates what can be achieved with an inspired planting

JOHN HAMMOND

There is little point in attempting to describe all that was accomplished over the next twenty one years – suffice it to say that once the years of neglect had been dealt with, there is hardly an area of the garden that wasn't altered in some way – by cutting of new paths and beds, the construction of stone walls, the excavating of new ponds, drainage work, and of course the introduction of new plants, most importantly rhododendrons, although many other genera have been planted, particularly those from areas with a high rainfall.

At the author's request in 1991, George F Smith wrote an excellent article in liaison with the Wright Brothers that details the wide range of rhododendrons to be found at Arduaine and this is recommended as further reading.[13] After much meditation over the difficult subject as to how to secure the future of the garden, Ed and Harry decided that the only realistic option was to gift Arduaine to the National Trust for Scotland (NTS) and, whilst the Brothers had some concerns about this course of action, the handover took place in early 1992. Achieving this object was no easy task as Diarmid Campbell, Inverawe Campbell family historian, recalls:[1]

Considerable work was done by two of Arthur's grandsons in convincing the NTS to consider the garden seriously: Sir Hugh Campbell-Byatt and his brother RA Campbell Byatt, both retired diplomats living in Argyll. Their mother Olga, Lady Byatt was Arthur's only daughter.

Maurice Wilkins was appointed as Property Manager/Head Gardener, but his attempts to liaise with the Wright Brothers came to naught. A few years earlier the Wright Brothers had built a new house, Arduaine Lodge, on a bluff above the garden entrance and its location provided an excellent view of the garden. Ed and Harry retained Arduaine Lodge, together with its separate area of garden, and thus were able to monitor the way of approach of the NTS in regard to managing the garden, which not surprisingly,

was in many ways markedly different to their own and contrary to their expectations. And sadly, as the months passed, a major rift developed between the Wright Brothers and the NTS concerning a number of issues. On the one hand, one could have some sympathy for Ed and Harry who strove for perfection in the creation of a woodland garden; on the other hand the NTS had limited resources and an inbuilt drive to do things in their own time and in their own way. Suffice it to say that many of the contentious issues are in the past and, central to the problems on both sides, has been a lack of communication, an unwillingness to admit that things could have been done differently, and a determination not to be seen to compromise. It has been a hard lesson for all concerned, including many observers who have come to realise only too clearly the reality that, from the date a property has been 'gifted', the future of the property is completely outwith the control of those who made the gift, irrespective of what may have been agreed prior to the handover taking place. And, in the case of a garden, the new 'owners' will inevitably want to make their own mark on the property. Sadly, Harry Wright passed away suddenly in late 1996; he was nearly 80.

Fifteen years on from the time the NTS took over the garden, Maurice Wilkins is still in the driving seat and caring for the garden he has always had a great affection for. It is to Maurice's credit that he has quietly maintained a high standard in respect of managing the upkeep of the garden in a way that continues to suggest private ownership, gradually making the inevitable changes that become necessary with the passing years as mature plantings begin to decline, and has continued the long tradition of entering trusses in Scotland's National Rhododendron Show. With a view to attracting visitors throughout the year Maurice has taken steps to introduce a wider range of plant material; however, this is being done with care and in sympathy with the existing plantings in the garden. In 1996 Maurice wrote the text of a very

HERE AT THE EAST end of the Cliff Path there are a number of zig-zags and a wide variety of interesting plants

JOHN HAMMOND

useful and well-illustrated guidebook to the garden, which he has updated several times since; this is available from the NTS.[14]

It was Gillie Mackie Campbell who on reflection said, *"It seems very odd to be talking about my recollections of Arduaine as though it is history. It doesn't feel like history. It feels like yesterday!"* And, despite the impact of nature and man across eleven decades of development, Arduaine remains one of Argyll's most romantic gardens, a magical garden planted with great skill and perception that continues to be visited by groups of horticultural enthusiasts from all over the world.

ACKNOWLEDGEMENTS
This article would have not come to fruition without the generous support of senior members of the Campbell Family who have shared memories, anecdotes and records connected with Arduaine House and Garden that stretch back to pre-Victorian days. In particular the author would like to thank Gillie Mackie Campbell of Stonefield House, Tarbert, who has been a friend for many years and has co-ordinated the input from family members; Diarmid Campbell of Kilmelford, family historian of the Inverawe Campbells, whose comments and suggestions have provided a more comprehensive perspective of J Arthur Campbell and his descendants; and Robin A Campbell-Byatt of Lochgilphead, who has provided details relating to William Hooker and the staff at Arduaine during WWII. I am also indebted, firstly, to Jean Maskell, Ardkinglas Estate, who has provided information about the Brennan Family; secondly to Maurice Wilkins, NTS Property Manager/Head Gardener at Arduaine, who has been most helpful and also made a transcript of the relevant notes written by James Arthur Campbell in his Arduaine Estate Journal; and finally to Edmund and Harry Wright, whose articles, letters and enclosures have helped outline their mammoth task of restoring the garden.

References ■ 1. Campbell, Diarmid (2007). Correspondence with the author re. Auchendarroch, Arduaine and the Inverawe Campbell Family. 2. Anon (2004). *The History of Kilmory*, Argyll and Bute Council, Kilmory Castle, Lochgilphead. 3. Campbell-Byatt, Robin A (2007). Correspondence with Diarmid Campbell re. Arduaine, Kilmory and William Hooker. 4. Campbell, Sir Ilay (1966). The Gardens at Arduaine, *RHS Rhododendron and Camellia Yearbook*, (1966). 5. Anon. *Clan McIver History*, Clan McIver Society, Strathendry Castle, Fife. 6. Campbell, James Arthur (1903–1929). Arduaine Estate Journal, Campbell Family archives. 7. *An Inventory of Gardens and Designed Landscapes in Scotland* (1987), Countryside Commission for Scotland, and Historic Buildings and Monuments Directorate, Scottish Development Department. 8. Wright, EAT (1994–1995). Correspondence with, and documents sent to, the author re. Arduaine Garden. 9. Maskell, Jean (2007). Correspondence with the author re. the Brennan Family. 10. Mackie Campbell, Gillie (1996–2007). Correspondence with the author re. Stonefield Castle and Arduaine. 11. Wright, EAT and Wright, HC undated. *Catalogue of Shrubs and Trees*, Royal Oak Nurseries, Cranham, Essex. 12. Wright, Edmund AT (1978). Arduaine Revived. *RHS Rhododendrons with Magnolias and Camellias*, (1979/80). 13. Smith, George F (2001). Arduaine: A Great Scottish Rhododendron Garden. *Journal, American Rhododendron Society*, Vol. 46, No. 1, Winter 1992: 55. 14. Wilkins, Maurice (1996–2002). *Arduaine Garden*, National Trust for Scotland, Edinburgh, (2002). 15. Wilkins, Maurice (2007). Correspondence with the author re. Arduaine Garden.

John Hammond *is a long standing member of the RCM Group and was Director at Large for the American Rhododendron Society for many years*

Who do you grow?

MALCOLM NASH

WHEN WE ADMIRE THE FRESH BEAUTY of our rhododendrons, magnolias and camellias each year, the sense of wonderment always affects us, just as it did the very first time we saw them, possibly quite a few seasons ago. Sometimes we may pause and ask our companions about the person after whom the plant was named, usually confess that we don't know but must look it up sometime, then walk on to be beguiled by the beauty of the next plant.

The editor asked me to begin a compilation of 'Who do you grow?', as an aide-memoire for such passing moments of curiosity. Many plants were named after 'gentry' who were good customers of the nurserymen; others to commemorate members of the raiser's families or to record important historical figures. Some descriptions may already be known by some members but it is hoped that most of the following will be of general interest.

Alice Martineau/Mrs PD Martineau The following detail has been kindly provided by Mrs Philip Martineau (wife of grandson, Cdr Philip Martineau) and is interesting enough to relay in full: *"In the 1930s, Mrs PD (Alice) Martineau had built several houses in the Sunningdale and Windlesham area and 'made' the gardens. During that time she bought from and made friends with the Slocock family and two of their pink seedlings were named after her. Mrs Martineau became Lady Martineau when her husband was knighted. She was a keen gardener and designed many gardens, including one for Queen Marie of Rumania and in Boston USA. She also wrote several gardening books."*

Alice Street Aunt of Frederick John Street. Miss Street died in 1953.

Alison Johnstone Late wife of George H Johnstone of Trewithen, a founder member of the Rhododendron Society.

Alma-Tadema Sir Lawrence Alma-Tadema, 1836–1912. Dutch-English painter of studies of Greek and Roman life.

Anne (Margaret) George Mrs Arthur George of Hydon Nurseries, Godalming, Surrey. Expert in antique porcelain and knowledgeable plantswoman.

Anne Rosse Daughter of Leonard and Maud Messel, mother of Lord Snowdon. Also a keen plantswoman who maintained a close interest in Nymans after the National Trust took over in 1953. Founder of the Victorian Society.

Arthur Bedford (Mr A Bedford) Head Gardener at Exbury 1925–1934.

Arthur J Ivens 1897–1954. Mr Ivens became General Manager at Hillier & Sons from 1946–1954. He wrote much of the manuscript for *The Hillier Manual of Trees and Shrubs*.

Arthur Osborn 1878–1964. Began his horticultural career at Kew in 1899 and became its Assistant Curator and Deputy Curator of the arboretum. Wrote two books, including the comprehensive *Trees and Shrubs for the Garden* (1933).

Barbara Hillier Lady Hillier, d. 2006. Wife of Sir Harold Hillier (1905–1985) of Hillier Nurseries, Winchester and donor of the Hillier Arboretum, Romsey.

Baron Schroder Baron Bruno Schroder. Born Hamburg 1867. Partner in J Henry Schroder Merchant Bank. Leading orchid grower and benefactor of the RHS – major financier of the building of the Old Horticultural (Lindley) Hall, Westminster. Lived latterly at Dell Park, Englefield Green, Surrey. Died 1940.

Bernard Crisp Son of Sir Frank Morris Crisp. Started Wargrave Plant Farm (mainly rock and alpine plants) at Twyford, Berks in about 1911. Became a director of John Waterer, Sons and Crisp when his nursery amalgamated with the Bagshot firm in 1914.

Brumas Celebrated polar bear cub at London Zoo around the time of naming the rhododendron in 1960.

Caractacus Ancient British Chieftain who tried to resist the Romans in 43–50 AD. Probably named because the horse 'Caractacus' won the Derby in 1862.

Caroline de Zoete A member of the stockbroking family. Was a student at Mrs Anne George's antiques firm.

Cetewayo King of the Zulus, defeated the British at Isandh-lwana but was defeated at Ulundi (1879). Was reinstated as ruler of part of Zululand. Died 1884.

Chandleri Elegans Alfred Chandler, 1804–1896. Nurseryman at Vauxhall, London. Renowned for camellias from about 1806 when his father began hybridising them.

Charles Noble Partner with John Standish, at Sunningdale, Berks. The firm of Standish and Noble endured from 1846 until 1856. Thereafter the nursery at Sunningdale was run by Noble only, until 1898.

Charles Rogier Charles Latour Rogier, 1800–1885. Frenchman who was the prime mover for the setting up of the Belgian state. He eventually became Prime Minister of Belgium, as did Hubert Frère-Orban who was not a monk, as his name suggests!

C.I.S. Claude I Sersanous of Portland, Oregon. President of the American Rhododendron Society in its early years (late 1940s and 1950s) Not Charles Ignatius Sargent, as one sometimes sees!

Clara Butt Dame Clara Butt, 1873–1976. Distinguished operatic contralto.

Colonel FR Durham Lt Col Frank Rogers Durham, 1872–1947. Secretary of the RHS 1926–1945.

Colonel Rogers Lt Col J M Rogers lived at Riverhill, Sevenoaks, Kent and was a member of the Rhododendron Association in the 1930s.

Corneille Pierre Corneille, 1606–1684. Regarded as founder of French classical drama.

Countess of Athlone HRH Princess Alice, 1883–1981.

Cynthia Another name for Artemis, virginal goddess of hunting and the moon (Greek mythology).

David Elder son of Lord (Stuart) Swaythling. He became the 4th Baron on the death of his father in 1990.

Dona Herzilia de Freitas Magalhaes Wife of Senhor de Freitas Magalhaes who raised the camellia from seed in 1925. A descendant of Ferdinand Magellan (Magalhaes).

Duchess of Portland Wife of 6th Duke of Portland, 1857–1943.

Duchess of Teck HRH Princess Mary of Cambridge.

Elsa Crisp Wife of Bernard Crisp *q.v.*

Etta Burrows The Burrows family were friends of Hjalmar Larson. They lived at Lakewood, south of Tacoma, Wash. Hjalmar named this seedling for Mrs Burrows who died in the mid 1980s.

Faggetter's Favourite Ted Faggetter was a Rhododendron foreman at Goldsworth Nursery.

Fénelon François Fénelon 1651–1715. Archbishop of Cambrai: theologian and writer. One of his works, *The Adventures of Telemaque* was regarded as a criticism of the government of Louis XIV.

Furnivall's Daughter Seedling of Mrs Furnivall whose persona did not have a daughter but Henry Goude, the Knap Hill nursery manager in the 1950s decided to name it thus because of the likeness to the parent.

Gauntlettii Raised by the V N Gauntlett & Co Nursery of Redruth, Cornwall and latterly of Chiddingfold, Surrey.

General Wavell 1883–1950. Highly distinguished soldier who became Field Marshal Earl Wavell.

General Sir John Du Cane Sir John Philip Ducane (apparently not Du Cane), 1865–1947. Eminent soldier of the Boer and First World Wars.

Gladys Lady Swaythling, 1879–1965. Wife of 2nd Lord Swaythling of Townhill Park, Swaythling, Southampton.

Hammondii Possibly raised by Edward Hammond at the Windlesham Nursery at Coopers Green near Bagshot in the first half of the 19th century.

Hydie Mr WGT (George) Hyde. Nurseryman of Ferndown, Dorset. Bred rhododendrons, deciduous and evergreen azaleas, many of which have been named and introduced by his daughter, Mrs Rosemary Legrand since her father died in 1980.

Hydon Rodney Rodney Longhurst is Arthur George's right hand man at Hydon Nurseries, and has been so for the past 46 years.

Hyperion An ancient Greek mythical god, son of Uranus and Gaea; father of Helios (sun), Selene (moon) and Eos (dawn).

Ivery's Scarlet Raised by Messrs Ivery of Dorking, Surrey.

Jacksonii Raised by the William Jackson & Co Nursery of Bedales, Yorkshire, about 1845.

James Burchett Mr Burchett was Mr WC Slocock's first foreman at Goldsworth Nursery from the beginning, c. 1879 until his retirement in 1931.

James Mangles James Henry Mangles, 1832–1884. Lived at Valewood, Haslemere, Surrey. Latterly Chairman of The London and South Western Railway Company. Raised fine *griffithianum* hybrids.

Janet Blair An American singer with the Hal Kemp band who appeared in several films, on stage and television in the USA. She died in February 2007, aged about 85.

Jill Dolding Wife of Stanley Dolding, retired horticultural adviser at Hillier Nurseries and sister of the late John Bond, former Keeper of the Valley and Savill Gardens, Windsor.

Jock (PH) Brydon Nurseryman and rhododendron enthusiast of Salem, Oregon. Committee member of the ARS in its early years.

J (John) Jennings Head Gardener to Leopold de Rothschild at Gunnersbury Park, West London in the 1920s.

John (Jock) Coutts 1872–1952. Kew 1896–1900, Head Gardener at Killerton 1900–1909, thence back to the Royal Botanic Gardens, Kew where he rose to become a distinguished curator from 1932–1937.

John Walter 1873–1968. Chairman of Directors of The Times Newspapers 1910–1923.

Joseph Whitworth Midlands industrialist and philanthropist who lived at Darley Dale, Derbyshire. Died 1897.

Lady Annette de Trafford Sister of Sir Humphrey de Trafford *q.v.*

Lady Bessborough Wife of 9th Earl of Bessborough, (1880–1956). Lady Bessborough was Roberte, daughter of Baron Jean de Neuflize.

Lady Clementine Mitford (1854–1932). Wife of 1st Baron Redesdale and daughter of 5th Earl of Airlie. Grandmother to 'The Mitford Girls' and aunt of the late Hon Angus Ogilvy.

Lady Decies Wife of 4th Baron Decies, (1865–1910).

SIR EDWARD CHARLES STIRLING with Rhododendron 'Mrs EC Stirling' at St Vigeans, Adelaide c.1905-10
INSET: Mrs EC Stirling

© ANNA POPE 2007

Lady Grey Egerton Wife of Sir Philip Grey Egerton who was a Council member of the RHS in the 1850s.

Lady Longman Wife of Sir Hubert Longman, the publisher who owned Sunningdale Nursery from 1905–1939.

Lady Vansittart Wife of 1st Baron Vansittart who was a diplomat and author, 1881–1957.

Leonard Messel 1872–1953. Dedicated plantsman and owner of Nymans, Sussex. Proprietor of family stockbroking firm. Was member of RHS Council and holder of VMH.

Lord Roberts 1832–1914. Had a distinguished military career in India and the Boer War.

Lord Fairhaven Major Henry Broughton, 2nd Baron Fairhaven d.1973. Created the fine woodland and water garden at South Walsham Hall, Norfolk where there is a collection of rhododendrons and azaleas.

Marion Street Second wife of the late Frederick John Street, well-known writer and nurseryman of the former Heathermead Nursery, West Chobham, Surrey.

Mary Swaythling First wife of 3rd Lord (Stuart) Swaythling.

Maud Messel Wife of Leonard Messel, *q.v.* 1876–1960. Very fond of herbaceous plants, roses and other scented plants.

Maxwell T Masters/Dr Masters MD FRS 1833–1907. Medical practitioner and editor of the *Gardeners' Chronicle* for many years. Also author of many botanical works.

Michael Rosse 6th Earl of Rosse, 1907–1979. 2nd husband of Anne Messel. A dedicated plantsman and head of many august bodies, including Deputy Chairman of the National Trust and a Vice-Chairman of the RHS.

Minnie Daughter of Charles Noble, *q.v.*

Mme Bertin Wife of M Bertin, nurseryman of Versailles, whose nursery was taken over by the Moser family in the late 19th century.

Mme Jules Porges Wife of Jules Porges who was a diamond merchant and brother of banker (Ephrussi Porges Bank) in Paris, 19th century.

Mrs AC Kenrick Wife of A Colin Kenrick who was a keen plantsman in the first half of the twentieth century. The Kenricks lived in several homes with gardens by Gertrude Jekyll.

Mrs Anthony Seys Mrs Anthony (Rosemary) Seys is the sister of Mr Edmund de Rothschild.

Mrs Charles E Pearson Wife of Charles Pearson, VMH, who was a partner in the firm of JR Pearson and Sons of Lowdham Notts. He was a founder member of the Horticultural Trade Association and member of the Floral Committee for 40 years. He died in 1929.

Mrs EC Stirling Wife of Sir Edward Charles Stirling (1848–1919) who was an eminent surgeon and scientist, knighted in 1917. Both hailed from South Australia.

Mrs Furnivall Cousin of Anthony Waterer of Knap Hill Nursery.

Mrs GW Leak Wife of GW Leak. Mr Leak was manager of Nurseryman RH Bath Ltd of Wisbech, Cambs, in the early 20th century.

Mrs Harry White Wife of Harry White who was manager of Sunningdale Nursery from 1898 until 1938.

Mrs JC Williams Wife of JC Williams of Caerhays, founder member of the Rhododendron Society.

Mrs John Kelk Probably named after Mrs John Kelk, wife of Sir John Kelk who was created Baronet in 1874 and died in 1923.

Mrs John Russell Wife of John Louis Russell (1897–1976), of LR Russell Ltd – Richmond and Windlesham Nurseries.

Mrs PD Williams Wife of PD Williams of Lanarth, Cornwall, founder member of the Rhododendron Society.

Mrs R S Holford Mr RS Holford was the founder of Westonbirt Arboretum.

Mrs W T Thiselton-Dyer Frances, wife of Sir William Turner Thiselton-Dyer. Sir William (1843–1928) was appointed Director of RBG Kew in 1899 and knighted in that year. He retired in 1905.

Mrs William Agnew Probably named after the wife of Sir William Agnew, who was born in 1825, knighted in 1895 and died in 1910. He was Chairman of Bradbury, Agnew and Co, printers, publishers and proprietors of *Punch* magazine.

Nancy Waterer Real name Ann Waterer, born 1853, daughter of Anthony Waterer snr, of Knap Hill Nursery.

Naomi Youngest daughter of Lionel de Rothschild and sister of Edmund de Rothschild.

Norma The protagonist of the opera by Bellini.

Olga Wife of the late Mr Oliver Slocock of Goldsworth Nursery, Woking, Surrey and mother of Mr Martin Slocock VMH, a Vice President of the RHS.

Quentin Metsys 1466–1530. Flemish painter who lived in Antwerp, noted for his portraits and scenes of everyday life.

Robert Keir Head Gardener to John Barr Stevenson of Tower Court, Ascot, Berks. His wife was Beatrice Keir.

Romy Mrs EG Millais, wife of the late Ted Millais, plant explorer and founder of Millais Nurseries Churt, Surrey.

Rosa Bonheur Marie-Rosalie Bonheur, 1822–1899. Painter and sculptor, especially of animals. Noted for remarkable accuracy and detail.

Russellianum Raised by Russell's nursery of Battersea, London in the 1850s.

Sappho Ancient Greek poetess of Lesbos.

Semiramis The legendary founder of Babylon; Wife of Ninus, king of Assyria, which she ruled with great skill after his death.

Sesostris King of Egypt who brought great prosperity to the country – 20th century BC.

Sigismund Rucker In the 19th century was well-known amateur gardener with a collection of orchids and ferns in his garden at Wandsworth, London. Died 1875.

Sir Humphrey de Trafford 1862–1929. Sportsman and noted breeder of horses.

Sir John Ramsden Sir John William Ramsden, Bt, 1831–1914. Parliamentarian of numerous addresses, including Bulstrode Park, near Gerrards Cross, Bucks. Sir John F Ramsden was a member of the Rhododendron Association in the 1930s.

Sully Duke of Sully, 1559–1641. French statesman who helped restore the finances of France in reign of Henri IV.

The Honourable Jean Marie de Montague Jean-Mary Montagu, daughter of Lord (Stuart) Swaythling. Not related to the Montagus of Beaulieu.

The Honourable Joyce Montague Joyce Montagu, born 1908. Sister of Lord (Stuart) Swaythling and aunt of Jean-Mary.

Towardii Named after Andrew Toward, 1796–1881. Was Head Gardener to the Duke of Gloucester at Bagshot Park, Surrey in the early 19th century, then became agent and farm bailiff to Queen Victoria at Osborne House, 1845–1871.

WE Gumbleton 1840–1911. Dilettante and enthusiastic gardener. Grew rare plants where he lived in Belgrove, Co. Cork, Ireland. He bequeathed his botanical library to the National Botanic Gardens, Glasnevin.

It became fashionable for rhododendrons to be named after racehorses, probably because horseracing was (and still is, of course) a popular sport across the spectrum of society. The following rhododendrons were winners of the Derby: Bahram 1935, Blue Peter 1939, Cameronian 1931, Crepello 1957, Doncaster 1873, Galceador 1950, Kettledrum 1861, Mahmoud 1936, Nimbus 1949, Sefton 1878, Tulyar 1952 and Windsor Lad 1934. Sun Chariot won the 1000 Guineas at Newmarket in 1942. Winners of the St Leger were: Marie Stuart 1873, Memoir 1890 and Rayon D'Or 1879.

The foregoing is a partly random and partly subjective selection of names but one that, it is hoped, will provide the beginning of a basis for quick reference or for deeper research. Of course, many more names could be added in future yearbooks, perhaps building to a comprehensive lexicon. Input from our international members would be of great value.

Malcolm Nash *is a long standing member of the Group, and has a particular interest in the conservation of deciduous azaleas*

Editor's Note

For the last few years new registrations of rhododendrons include the derivation of the chosen name but for the vast majority of entries in the Register this is obviously not the case.

The Registrar, Alan Leslie, is keen to see this information incorporated if available, so that the record is as informative and complete as possible. The International Rhododendron Register is so much more than a description of a hybrid – it is also a social and historical record of the people, places and events of the time of naming. By including this article, it is hoped that information will start to flow so that when the Register goes online, rhododendron growers will know 'who they grow'!

Notes on the cultivation, morphology and nomenclature of eleven hardy Asian evergreen magnolias

RICHARD B FIGLAR

IT WAS THE FAMOUS North American evergreen magnolia, *Magnolia grandiflora*, which sparked my intense interest in this genus 33 years ago. Shortly after that, I vividly remember the excitement I felt when I opened George Johnstone's *Asiatic Magnolias in Cultivation* and first read about the exotic *Magnolia nitida* and the spectacular *M. delavayi*, the two important Chinese counterparts to our own *M. grandiflora*. As time went by, my curiosity about these and other Asian evergreen magnolias intensified, but *M. delavayi* and the other species in section *Gwillimia* were considered far too tender, and *M. nitida* was all but impossible to obtain. So I settled for growing *M. delavayi* and *M. coco* in pots inside my home which at the time was Pomona, New York. At the same time I also became acquainted with the, then, magnolia-like relatives, *Michelia* and *Manglietia* but information and literature regarding them was sparse to non-existent.

Things changed rapidly by the middle 1990s. Names like *Michelia maudiae* and *Manglietia fordiana* began to appear in nursery catalogues, and scientists, using DNA sequencing, were becoming increasingly convinced that these genera were indeed part of *Magnolia* after all.

Today, while we are still in the process of getting used to their new names in *Magnolia*, for the taxa of the former genera *Michelia* and *Manglietia*, the demand for many of these 'new' evergreen magnolias continues to grow rapidly. It's not surprising, since many – perhaps a dozen species – are fairly easy to grow here in southeastern US as well as in parts of western Europe, the UK, Australia, NZ and in other warm-temperate parts of the world. Although generally not as showy in flower as the popular deciduous species and hybrids of section *Yulania*, these Asian evergreen magnolias provide something distinctly different – and sometimes stunningly ornamental – in magnolia expression for our gardens.

In this report, I will discuss my experiences in cultivating eleven of the most cold-hardy Chinese evergreen magnolias in southeastern US; five each from sections *Michelia* and *Manglietia*, and one from section *Gynopodium*. Besides providing information on plant culture, performance and ornamental potential, I hope to convey some useful details of their individual morphologies since there are still many lingering problems in the marketplace, and in science, regarding the correct identification and names of many of these taxa. Undoubtedly, some of this has been due to simple mislabeling or misidentification on the part of those exporters/importers in the

These Asian evergreen magnolias provide something distinctly different – and sometimes stunningly ornamental

nursery supply chain. But in other cases it came about by the naming of some taxa more than once by two (or more) taxonomists, or in a few cases by a single taxonomist having unintentionally assigned two different names to two separate collections of the same species. This is understandable, since sometimes collections were incomplete or not ideally representative of the plants they were collected from. Evidently, such was the case with a few of James Dandy's names. To make matters worse, since taxonomists outside of southeast Asia sometimes had little or no familiarity with *Michelia* and *Manglietia*, there may have been inadequate peer review for some proposed species before their names were published.

Recently, Chen & Nooteboom (1993), Li Jie (1997), Sima Yong-Kang (2001), Sima *et al.*

(2002, 2003), V. Sampath Kumar (2006) and others have made some inroads into resolving some of these problems. But much more work remains to be done.

Here, I will attempt to justify each taxon with key morphological characters while providing relevant nomenclatural and taxonomical history where required. Since comparatively little information has been assembled in the literature about these taxa and their cultivation, this report should be regarded as preliminary.

The eleven taxa selected have been growing in many parts of the southeastern US and in my own test garden, *Magnolian Grove Arboretum* (MGA), which is located more or less on the border of USDA zone 7b/8a just south of the Blue Ridge Mountains near Clemson in western South Carolina. Our annual coldest temperature averages about −10°C (13°F), but temperatures at

TYPICAL BLOOM of *Magnolia maudiae*

RICHARD FIGLAR

or slightly below −18°C (0°F) have occurred 2 or 3 times in the past 50 years. Summers are warm with the average daily maximum and minimum for July being about 32°C (90°F) and 20°C (68°F). This temperature profile is very similar to what is experienced along a line from Norfolk, Virginia; Raleigh, North Carolina; Atlanta, Georgia, to Birmingham, Alabama. However, our proximity to the mountains results in an average of 60 inches annual rainfall which is somewhat greater than the average totals for those cities.

MAGNOLIA MAUDIAE in full bloom on January 8, 2007 at South Carolina Botanical Garden

RICHARD FIGLAR

MAGNOLIA MAUDIAE

Formerly referred to the genus *Michelia*, *Magnolia maudiae* is now placed in section *Michelia* of the subgenus *Yulania*. Although it may not seem obvious to the casual observer, there are many morphological characters which section *Michelia* has in common with the familiar deciduous species in section *Yulania* of subgenus *Yulania*: The stamens spread and remain attached to the androphore long after the blooms have completed their sexual function; blooms are produced mainly precociously, that is, during late winter or early spring usually before new vegetative growth appears; and flowers are often positioned on abbreviated branchlets emerging from leaf axils of the previous year's growth – almost always in section *Michelia*, occasionally in section *Yulania* (especially in *M. stellata*).

In cultivation *Magnolia maudiae* forms a rounded, slightly open tree of about 30 feet in height. It blooms here in early February but sometimes as early as late December or January if a string of abnormally warm days occurs. The pure white, nine tepaled flowers are fairly large – to 6 inches in diameter when opened flat – and have a magnificent fragrance which reminds me of gardenia, but better. Even fairly young trees, one or two meters tall, can produce blooms. Leaves are slightly leathery, of oblong shape, with short blunt apices and obtuse bases. Leaf backs are slightly glaucous, which imparts a superficial resemblance to *Magnolia virginiana*, but unlike that species, *M. maudiae* has little or no visible stipular scar on the leaf petiole. Most important, *Magnolia maudiae* can easily be separated from the other michelias presented here in that all parts of the plant are completely glabrous [note: with a hand lens, short rufous hairs can sometimes be seen on the apices of flower buds]. Perhaps for this reason there are no taxonomic or nomenclature problems for *M. maudiae* at this time.

M. maudiae is arguably the most ornamental magnolia presented here, however, its wintertime blooming season means that it will always be problematic in most of southeastern US and perhaps other areas as well. Unlike other winter blooming magnolias such as *M. zenii*, whose open blooms can remain undamaged even after several degrees of frost, the blooms of *M. maudiae* are intolerant of even the slightest frost. Given its wide distribution in south and SE China, from Zhejiang and Fujian provinces in the east to Guangxi and Guizhou in the west, it is possible that there is enough natural variation for later blooming individuals of *M. maudiae* to exist. I have just begun to test one clone which is said to be later (March) blooming.

MAGNOLIA PLATYPETALA (ined.)

This michelia was reduced to, the then, *Michelia cavaleriei* by Chen & Nooteboom in 1993. In 2001, Sima Yong-Kang proposed it as a variety of *Magnolia maudiae*. No doubt, all three of these former *Michelia* species – *M. cavaleriei*, *M. maudiae*, and *M. platypetala* – are closely related, but in my view *M. platypetala* is sufficiently distinct to be maintained as a separate species. [Thus, I refer to it above as

'ined.' since the name *Magnolia platypetala* has not been published as yet.] This taxon does indeed resemble *M. maudiae*, however its young twigs, buds, young leaves, peduncles and petioles are covered with fine reddish-brown sericeous hairs. Its leaves are also oblong in shape and of similar size, 10–15cm long by 3–5cm wide, but seem to have mostly acuminate apices. Its flowers are similar to those of *M. maudiae* – nine pure white tepals and it blooms at the same early date – however the plant is generally less floriferous, and the blooms are slightly smaller and less fragrant than those of *M. maudiae* in plants that I have seen. In cultivation it would be of similar landscape size as *M. maudiae*. Growing at 1000–1500m elevations from western Hubei southward to northeast Guangxi, its range in China is more restrictive than that of *M. maudiae* but it is positioned farther to the north. This would suggest that *M. platypetala* is more cold-hardy than *M. maudiae* which could indeed be the case. *M. platypetala* could also be confused with *M. macclurei* (which is not discussed here) but the latter species has rhombic-elliptic leaves with acute to, at most, short-acuminate leaf apices.

MAGNOLIA CAVALERIEI

I received this plant mislabeled, as *Michelia fulgens*, many years ago, but it is quite clear that it belongs to *Magnolia cavaleriei*. As mentioned

THE ATTRACTIVE FLOWER BUDS of *Magnolia platypetala*, South Carolina Botanical Garden, Clemson

RICHARD FIGLAR

MAGNOLIA CAVALERIEI blooming at Piroche Plants, Pitt Meadows, BC

RICHARD FIGLAR

before, there is no doubt that this species is very closely related to *M. platypetala*. In fact, I find it difficult to separate them based on the written descriptions given for them in *Magnolias of China* (Liu *et al.*, 2004). But in cultivation it is easy to notice the much larger – mostly 15–20cm long – but distinctly narrower leaves of this species. It has similar sericeous hairs on the same parts of the plant, but unlike *M. platypetala*, the pubescence in *M. cavalerei* is much lighter in colour, from silver-gray to pale brown. Also, its twigs at 4mm in diameter are stouter than the 2mm twigs of *M. platypetala*. Its abundantly produced, well formed, white flowers each consist of 12 tepals instead of 9in the previous two species. Un-fortunately, *M. cavaleriei* is also very precocious, producing blooms normally in late January and early February here. In fact, because of the high incidence of freezes during that mid-winter blooming period, I have never seen it bloom to perfection here at Magnolian Grove. *M. cavaleriei's* distribution is positioned to the west of the previous two species, from northwest Guangxi and part of Guizhou westward to southeastern Sichuan and southeastern Yunnan.

Dandy's *Michelia fallax* (1928) has long been considered synonymous with *M. cavaleriei*.

Though spectacular in bloom, all three of these species present serious limitations as useful ornamental plants in southeastern US since their mid-winter blooming occurs at a time when freezes are common and normal. In coastal regions as well as peninsular Florida, some of these limitations may be overcome by the much lower frequency of frost during winter at these milder locations. Here at Magnolian Grove, I hedge my bet by planting some *M. maudiae* on warmer south-facing sites while others are planted in colder 'frost pockets'. This way, if a sufficiently long warm spell occurs in mid-winter, it might be long enough to force bloom on the warm-sited plants, but if those are ruined, the cold-sited plants might be held back long enough to bloom successfully at a later, safer, date in March.

MAGNOLIA FOVEOLATA

Though most of the michelias normally bloom too early, a few do not – and one of these is *Magnolia foveolata*. This late March/early April blooming species is native to a vast area of South China: from Guangdong in the east to Yunnan in the west, while ranging as far north as Hubei and south as Hainan; and even

MAGNOLIA FOVEOLATA in Ha Giang province, Vietnam. Note the gynoecium protruding beyond the tips of the unopened tepals

STEVE HOOTMAN

DENSE INDUMENTUM on adaxial (top) side of a young leaf (Above)

AN AKIRA SHIBAMICHI selection of *Magnolia foveolata* showing lustrous golden indumentum on both sides of leaves (Above and Right)

MAGNOLIA FOVEOLATA at Magnolian Grove Arboretum

RICHARD FIGLAR

northern Vietnam. In concert with Dr Peter Wharton's opinion as expressed in *Davidsonia* recently (2006), I believe *Magnolia foveolata* is the most ornamental and exciting of the former *Michelia* species that we can grow here. Even if it weren't ever to flower, the leaves (both sides), twigs, buds, petioles, etc. are covered with abundant appressed indumentum in varying hues of gold to copper and silver, sometimes all three colors being expressed on various parts of the same plant. And unlike the celebrated red-brown indumentum of the American *Magnolia grandiflora*, which portrays the luster of a dull ink blotter, the glistening indumentum of *M. foveolata* literally shimmers in the sunlight. Sometimes the whole tree appears to be sprinkled with gold dust. In addition to all that, we also have in *Magnolia foveolata* a michelia that blooms late enough in the season to flower reliably here in southeastern US. Unlike the blooms of the previous species discussed, the 9–12 tepaled flowers of *M. foveolata* are mostly

pale yellow to creamy white in color and are distinctly cup-shaped after opening from a globe-like poise in which the gynoecium protrudes at the apex. The effect is quite stunning. The flowers appear to be about 3–4in (8–10cm) in diameter even though tepals can measure up to 7cm in length. The long, red filamented, stamens enhance the beauty of the flowers. The light flower fragrance reminds me of the fresh smell of sliced (canned) pears on a fruit salad.

It is unlikely that this species can be confused with any other; however, it is conceivable that young plants could be confused with *M. cavaleriei*, but the latter species has smaller, less coriaceous, leaves and is much less tomentose. Also, the stipules of *M. foveolata* are more leathery than in any magnolia that I've seen. Plants with silver indumentum on the leaf-backs are often referred to as *M. foveolata* var. *cinerascens*. While this designation is useful and descriptive for horticulture, most botanists

THE PETITE FLOWER of *Magnolia laevifolia*

RICHARD FIGLAR

don't recognize this status. There are several synonyms for *M. foveolata*. The most important of these, *Michelia fulgens*, was reduced to *Michelia foveolata* fifteen years ago (BL Chen & Nooteboom, 1993) while *Michelia aenea* and *Michelia longistyla* were reduced to *Michelia foveolata* in 1997 (Li Jie, 1997). Later, all three synonyms were validated to belong to *Magnolia foveolata* (Sima *et al.*, 2003). So those who purchase plants under these names may be confident that they will be getting *Magnolia foveolata*, barring labeling mistakes, of course.

MAGNOLIA LAEVIFOLIA (*Magnolia dianica*)

This magnolia has been under cultivation under its former name, *Michelia yunnanensis*, for quite a long time but only for the past few years in the US. As with *M. foveolata*, *Magnolia laevifolia* has the dual advantage of being cold hardy (perhaps to colder parts of USDA zone 7) and it blooms fairly late in the season, late March to early April, here in southeastern US. But unlike all the previous species, *M. laevifolia* produces petite, bright

white blooms of just 2–3in (5–8cm) in diameter on a small-leaved tree (or large shrub) of just 4m tall. Because of its small size and ability to bloom at a young age, *Magnolia laevifolia* might have the greatest commercial potential for ornamental horticulture of any of the magnolias discussed here. Most individuals of *M. laevifolia* have a slightly straggly branching habit which I believe could easily be overcome via the selection process. One cultivar, 'Michelle', selected recently by Tony Avent of Plant Delights Nursery near Raleigh, NC is superior in form and flowering attributes. Many more cultivars are likely to follow.

Unfortunately, this taxon has been the victim of a couple of taxonomic and nomenclatural missteps. It was first named *Michelia yunnanensis* in 1906 by Finet & Gagnepan based on the description and name provided by the, then deceased, French botanist, Adrien Franchet (1884–1900). Nearly a century later, in 1988, the Chinese taxonomist, Professor Liu Yu-Hu (Law Yuh-Wu) and his associate YF Wu of the South China Institute of Botany described and named a similar taxon, *Michelia laevifolia*, from Anlong

MAGNOLIA LAEVIFOLIA 'Michelle' at Juniper Level Botanic Gardens, Raleigh, NC

RICHARD FIGLAR

THE LOVELY bi-coloured flower of *Magnolia insignis* (Piroche Group)

RICHARD FIGLAR

in Guizhou province. Shortly after that, BL Chen and Hans Nooteboom (1993) and others confirmed that *M. laevifolia* was actually the same taxon as *Michelia yunnanensis* and thus, reduced it to that species. Genus *Michelia* was reduced to *Magnolia* (Figlar, 2000), and since the epithet 'yunnanensis' had already been used for *Magnolia yunnanensis* of section *Gynopodium* (Nooteboom, 1985), I selected the next earliest available epithet, the synonym 'laevifolia', for the new combination. However, in doing so, I failed to make proper reference under the new name. So my name *Magnolia laevifolia* was rendered invalid. Having noticed this error and evidently thinking that the epithet 'laevifolia' was no longer available, Sima Yong-Kang proposed a new name, *Magnolia dianica*, for *Michelia yunnanensis*. This seemed the fitting solution, since the word "Dian" was the 3rd century BC name for what is now Yunnan. I agreed with Sima and he kindly included me as co-author of the new name (Sima, 2001). Now, it has been determined by the rules of the ICBN that the epithet laevifolia is indeed available, and that it, rather than dianica, is the earliest available name. During the time of writing, the new combination, *Magnolia laevifolia*, was published (Charlermglin & Nooteboom, 2007). As new names for familiar taxa are almost always unpopular and unwelcomed by horticulturists, I apologize for my role in this awkward and drawn-out name change.

MAGNOLIA INSIGNIS

Except for having four or more seeds per carpel, this species and others of the former genus *Manglietia* distinguish themselves little from other members of subgenus *Magnolia*. Indeed, DNA studies (Azuma *et al.*, 2001, 2004) and morphology (the whorl-like flush of new leaves produced on the branch tips) place this group as a 'sister' section (or clade) to section *Rhytidospermum*. Like most magnolias of subgenus *Magnolia*, their blooms appear in late spring or early summer – mostly after new vegetative growth has commenced – and the stamens detach and fall away from the androphore during the initiation of the male phase of the flower, which is usually the second day after the flower first opens. Since manglietias bloom at roughly the same time (May through July) as our native *Magnolia grandiflora*, these five species are very easy to cultivate here in the southeast.

By far, the most important of the hardy manglietia species discussed here are the red (or deep pink) flowering forms of *Magnolia insignis*. In the US, it appears that virtually all of these

MAGNOLIA INSIGNIS (Piroche Group) growing at MGA

RICHARD FIGLAR

a stunning display of 3 red and 3 white tepals – a sort of bicolor effect not seen in most magnolias. Interestingly, the pink or red pigment (to RHS 59C) is greatest at the apex of the tepals and least at the base, which is precisely the opposite of what is normally seen on pigmented tepals of subgenus *Yulania* species and hybrids. Occasionally, some individuals of the 'Piroche Group' produce entirely red pigmented blooms. The flowers, which have a sweet melon-like scent, are the most fragrant of the manglietias described here.

Various taxonomists have cited several synonyms for *Magnolia insignis*. These include *Manglietia shangpaensis*, *M. patungensis*, *M. tenuifolia*, and *M. maguanica*. The latter synonym, which produces red-pigmented flowers, is native to lower elevations of southeast Yunnan. Thus, it is possible that southeastern Yunnan could be the origin of the 'Piroche Group' *M. insignis*.

MAGNOLIA CONIFERA

Dandy named this species on account of its fruits looking "not unlike small pine-cones." This species was evidently named twice by Dandy based on two separate collections, the first (1930) from Son Tay province, Vietnam (*Manglietia conifera*) and one year

deep pigmented flower forms in cultivation were introduced via Piroche Plants of Pitt Meadows, BC in the 1990s. Perhaps, this was an amazing stroke of luck, since *M. insignis* more typically produces small, creamy white flowers – sometimes with only slight degrees of pink pigmentation on the outer tepals – through much of its extensive range which stretches from the western part of south China, to NE India, Nepal, to parts of Myanmar and northern Vietnam.

Plants of the 'Piroche Group' also seem to be more cold-hardy, easily remaining fully evergreen here at –14°C (6°F) while other seedlings of *M. insignis* were defoliated and/or suffered dieback in more moderate winters. The 9 tepaled blooms often measure 6 inches across when opened flat. When the flower buds first open (in the early evening), the greenish-red outer 3 tepals reflex downward and remain in that position, while the rest of the tepals open normally and usually provide

THE NODDING BLOOM of *Magnolia conifera* var. *chingii* at South China Botanical Garden, Guangzhou, China

ZENG QING-WEN

"ORCHARD" of *Magnolia conifera* in Xiangpingshan in SE Yunnan, China

RICHARD FIGLAR

later (1931) from Guangxi province, China (*Manglietia chingii*). When one reads the original Latin descriptions, it is surprising how alike they are. Much later, in 1997, Li Jie of the Kunming Institute of Botany proposed that the latter be retained as *Manglietia conifera* subsp. *chingii*, based on a few dimensional differences. VS Kumar echoed that reasoning when he renamed them *Magnolia conifera* and *M. conifera* var. *chingii* in 2006. This species grows naturally from Guangdong province in southeastern China, westward to Yunnan and northern Vietnam.

When I first saw this plant in 1998 in Kunming, I was astonished at how similar in size, form and poise the flowers are to those of *Magnolia sieboldii* and the others in section *Oyama*. Consisting of mostly eleven tepals, the flowers hang semi-pendulously from 6–9cm peduncles. Surrounding the green gynoecium of these small white, 3 inch (8cm) blooms is a boss of bright red-purple stamens.

Leaves are a lustrous dark green and thick – not too different from the consistency of those of

M. grandiflora – which makes *M. conifera* easy to distinguish from a young *M. insignis* on the nursery lot.

MAGNOLIA MOTO

Though hardy in our part of the southeastern US, *M. moto* is probably the least cold-hardy of the magnolias discussed here. I include it mainly because of the magnificent red-brown, villous indumentum which thickly covers the young twigs, buds, leaf midribs (abaxial side), petioles, and peduncles. Unlike the velvety, appressed indumentum of *M. foveolata,* the 1–2mm long hairs of *M. moto* grow perpendicular to the surface of the twig, bud, etc. Leaves are thinly coreaceous, obovate-elliptic in shape and measure about 18cm long by 6cm wide.

With its 6–12cm long peduncles, *M. moto* also produces pendulant, *M. sieboldii*-like, flowers that are 9 tepaled and somewhat larger (about 4 inches (10cm) across when open flat) than those of *M. conifera*. Dr Clifford Parks of Chapel Hill, NC was probably the first to introduce this species to the US in 1994. He has a tree of that original introduction in his collection that is now nearly 10m tall. As with some of the other

VILLOUS RED-BROWN indumentum adorns twigs, petioles and buds of *Magnolia moto* at MGA

RICHARD FIGLAR

PEDUNCLES and unopened flower bud of *Magnolia moto* reveal dense covering of red-brown pubescence   ZENG QING-WEN

LOOKING UP into the pendulant bloom of *Magnolia moto* at South China Botanical Garden ZENG QING-WEN

Chinese taxa discussed here, *M. moto* grows naturally from southern Fujian and Guangdong in the east, to southeast Yunnan in the west. Because of similar indumentum, *M. moto* could potentially be confused with *Magnolia megaphylla* and *M. dandyi* but those two species have short peduncles and much larger leaves. *Magnolia rufibarbata*, a comparable and possibly allied species from Vietnam, is also similar but it, too, lacks the long peduncle. At this time there aren't any obvious nomenclature issues regarding *M. moto*, but some researchers think it might be very similar, if not the same, as an earlier named taxon, *Manglietia kwangtungensis*, which is native to the same general area.

MAGNOLIA FORDIANA AND MAGNOLIA YUYUANENSIS

These two species are discussed together, since they probably have both been treated as *M. fordiana* after their introduction to North America during the 1980s. In contrast to the two previously discussed species, these produce larger (to 5in or 13cm when open flat), upward-facing white flowers but they are similar in that the gynoecium is subtended by a boss of bright red stamens.

Native to a vast area of south China from Anhui in the east to Yunnan and Vietnam in the west, *Manglietia fordiana* was named for Charles Ford, a British plant explorer of south China, in 1891. In 1924, the famous Chinese taxonomist, HH Hu – seemingly ahead of his time – renamed it *Magnolia fordiana*. Later (1985), another prominent Chinese taxonomist, Liu Yu-Hu (Law Yuh-Wu), assigned the name, *Manglietia yuyuanensis*, to what appears to be the populations of *M. fordiana* in the northeastern part of its range (Anhui, Zhejiang, etc.). Others such as Chen & Nooteboom (1993) did not recognize Liu's species. However, in 2006, in renaming the remaining former *Manglietia* spp., VS Kumar maintained *Magnolia yuyuanensis* based on its more glabrous plant parts, the color of the ripe twigs (yellowish brown vs. reddish-brown), the shape of the leaf apex (caudate or acuminate vs. acute), length of peduncle (15–20mm vs. 5–10mm), size of outer tepals (3.5–4cm long vs. 6–7cm long) and color of outer tepals (greenish and/or pinkish vs. pure white). Based on these differences and after examining specimens of these taxa grown in the US, I tend to support Liu's and now Kumar's position. In fact, it appears that most

MAGNOLIA FORDIANA at South China Botanical Garden   ZENG QING-WEN

plants marketed under the name *Magnolia fordiana* are actually *M. yuyuanensis*. Whether one considers them as two separate species or as varieties of *M. fordiana*, both are fairly unique among manglietias in that when viewed from the underside of the leaf, the lateral veins are indistinct, or barely discernable to the eye.

In the garden, both species are very effective as tropical-looking foliage subjects. With their long narrow leaves – often positioned in false whorls at the ends of the branches – the foliage of these impressive magnolias is evocative of the Mango Tree (*Mangifera indica*). In cultivation one should expect *M. fordiana* and *M. yuyuanensis* to perform in ultimate size and possibly hardiness much like its North American cousin, *M. grandiflora*.

MAGNOLIA LOTUNGENSIS (see front cover)

The last magnolia to be discussed here is this very cold-hardy member of section *Gynopodium*, *Magnolia lotungensis*. Being very closely related to the similar *Magnolia nitida* (and at one time considered a variety of it), *M. lotungensis* is distinguished from that species by its red pigmented stamens (instead of creamy-white) and by its wider distribution at lower (700–1400m) elevations throughout southern China. In contrast, *M. nitida* is limited to higher (1800–2500m) elevations comprising a small area of southeast Tibet, NW Yunnan and northern Myanmar. Curiously, some individuals of

MAGNOLIA YUYUANENSIS showing off its mango-like foliage in Aiken, South Carolina

RICHARD FIGLAR

MAGNOLIA YUYUANENSIS at South China Botanical Garden   ZENG QING-WEN

MAGNOLIA YUYUANENSIS at MGA showing pigmented outer tepals.

RICHARD FIGLAR

culture. Not only is it cold-hardy, it just may be the hardiest magnolia discussed here, with the possible exception of *M. yuyuanensis*. The only problem, so far, is that this species evidently takes a long time to reach sexual maturity. There are many plants in cultivation from Norfolk, Virginia to Raleigh, North Carolina – even in zone 6 near Kansas City, Kansas – to the 20 foot tall plant here at MGA, but none has flowered yet, to my knowledge.

Because all five species in section *Gynopodium*, including *M. lotungensis*, are totally glabrous, they could conceivably only be confused with *M. maudiae*. But the pseudo-axillary flower position and the larger, less glossy, leaves of the latter species allow for easy distinction between *M. maudiae* and *M. lotungensis*.

In Chinese taxonomy, since 1951, all the members of section *Gynopodium* were relegated to the genus *Parakmeria*. Although this taxonomic placement was never really recognized by western taxonomists, the use of

M. lotungensis (as well as two other species in this section) are androdioecious, that is, they produce only male flowers (having tepals and stamens, but no gynoecium). This androdioecious character has not been observed in *M. nitida*.

As a cultivated tree, *M. lotungensis* gives us yet another very different, but striking, expression of ornamental presentation in a magnolia for the garden: thick, highly polished, evergreen leaves in hues from crimson red (when young) to deep rich green. Moreover, these petite elliptical leaves normally measure just 5–10cm long by 2.5cm wide. In growth habit the tree is strikingly columnar, sometimes with a branch spread of only 5ft on a 20ft-tall tree. Although it is reported to be difficult (or impossible?) to root from cuttings, it grafts effortlessly on to understocks of *M.* x *loebneri* and *M. acuminata* and probably other members of section *Yulania* as well. It

THE POLISHED FOLIAGE of *Magnolia lotungensis* is enhanced by the red-tinted newly emerging leaves

RICHARD FIGLAR

grafts so reliably, that I've top-worked many of the wild *M. acuminata* seedlings that frequently volunteer on our property here in South Carolina.

To magnolia enthusiasts here in the southeast, who have long wished they could grow the very splendid but tender *M. nitida*, *M. lotungensis* represents a major breakthrough in magnolia

the generic name still persists in parts of China even today. Recently (2006), Lin Qi along with four other Chinese researchers (using the genus name *Parakmeria*) proposed that *M. lotungensis* and the closely related – but very rare – *Magnolia omeiensis* (endemic to Mount Emei in Sichuan) are one and the same species. Thus, they reduced *M. lotungensis* to a synonym of *M. omeiensis*. Based on the descriptions I have read for *Magnolia omeiensis*, this seems very plausible. If this argument proves successful, then both taxa will be absorbed under the older name, *M. omeiensis*.

Obviously, we are only beginning to scratch the surface of possibilities for ornamental horticulture with these eleven Asian evergreen magnolias. Even though a few, such as *Magnolia insignis*, have been in cultivation for quite a long time, hardly any cultivar selections have been made. Of the eleven, I think *M. insignis*, *M. foveolata*, *M. laevifolia* and *M. lotungensis* have the greatest

potential for widespread use in our gardens, but finding a later blooming *M. maudiae* would easily trump all those. The search doesn't stop. I am currently testing others here at MGA, including *M. floribunda*, *M. odora*, *M. macclurei*, *M. shiluensis*, *M. fulva*, *M. ernestii*, *M. lanuginosa* and *M. chapensis* (all of section *Michelia*); *M. ovoidea*, *M. crassipes* (syn. *Manglietia pachyphylla*), *M. megaphylla* (all three of section *Manglietia*); and *Magnolia sinica* (of subgenus *Gynopodium*) and there are several more that are yet to be introduced. Undoubtedly this is still a nascent effort. More surprises lie ahead, I'm sure.

Richard Figlar
is Past President of the Magnolia Society International

References ■ Azuma, H, García-Franco J, Rico-Gray, V and Thien, LB (2001). Molecular Phylogeny of the Magnoliaceae: The biogeography of tropical and temperate disjunctions. *Amer. J. Bot.* 88(12): 2275–2285. Azuma, H L, Rico-Gray, V, García-Franco, JG, Toyota, M, Asakawa, Y and Thien, LB (2004). *Acta Phytotax. Geobot.* 55(3): 167–180. Chalermglin, P & Nooteboom, HP (2007). A new species of and a new combination in *Magnolia* (Magnoliaceae). *Blumea* 52: 559–562.Chen, BL & Nooteboom, HP (1993). Notes on Magnoliaceae III: The Magnoliaceae of China. *Ann. Missouri Bot. Gard.* 80: 999–1104. Dandy, JE (1928). New or Noteworthy Chinese Magnoliaceae. *Notes Royal Bot. Gdn. Edinburgh* 16: 130–131. Dandy, JE (1930). New Magnolieae from China and Indo-China. *Jour. Bot.* 68: 205–206. Dandy, JE (1931). Four new Magnolieae from Kwangsi. *Jour. Bot.* 69: 232. Figlar, RB (2000). Proleptic branch initiation in *Michelia* and *Magnolia* subgenus *Yulania* provides basis for combinations in subfamily Magnolioideae. In: YH Liu *et al.* (eds.) *Proceedings Internat. Symp. Fam. Magnoliaceae 1998*: 14–25. Science Press, Beijing, China. Figlar, RB & Nooteboom, HP (2004). Notes on Magnoliaceae IV. *Blumea* 49: 87–100. Finet, EA & Gagnepain, F (1905–1906). Contributions à la flore de l'Asie orientale d'après l'herbier du muséum de Paris. *Bull. Soc. Bot. France* 52 (Mémoires 4): 44. Hu, HH (1924). Notes on Chinese ligneous plants. *J. of Arnold Arb.* 5: 228. Hu, HH & Cheng, WY (1951). *Parakmeria*, a new genus of Magnoliaceae of southwestern China. *Acta Phytotax. Sinica* 1: 1–2. Johnstone, GH (1955). *Asiatic Magnolias in Cultivation*. Royal Horticultural Society, London. Kumar, VS (2006). New combinations and new names in Asian *Magnoliaceae*. *Kew Bulletin* 61: 183-186. Li, J (1997). Some notes on Magnoliaceae from China. *Acta Bot. Yunnan.* 19(2): 131–138. Liu, YH (as Law, YW) (1985). *Bull. Bot. Res.* (China) 5(3): 125. Liu, YH (as Law, YW) & Wu, YF 1988. *Bull. Bot. Res.* (China) 8(3): 72. Liu, YH (Law, YW) ed.-in-chief; Zeng, QW, Zhou, RZ & Xing, FW asso. eds. (2004). *Magnolias of China*. Baitong Books, Beijing Science & Technology Press. Nooteboom, HP (1985). Notes on Magnoliaceae. *Blumea* 31: p. 88. Sima, YK (2001). Some Notes on *Magnolia* subgenus *Michelia* from China. *Yunnan Forestry Science & Technology*. No. 2: 29–35. Sima, YK and Chalermglin, P (2002). New data for Magnoliaceae plants in Yunnan province of China, Thailand and Vietnam. *Bull. Bot. Res.* (China) 22(3): 271–272. Sima, YK, Shui, YM & Chen, WH (2003). Magnoliaceae. In: YM Shui (ed.) *Seed plants of Honghe region in SE Yunnan, China. Kunming*: Yunnan Science and Technology Press: 53–56. Wharton, PA (2006). *Evergreen magnolias growing at UBC Botanical Garden, Vancouver, Canada: a progress report*: 116–133.

New evergreen magnolias: Comments from UK growers

MIKE ROBINSON, JOHN MARSTON & MAURICE FOSTER

EVERGREEN MAGNOLIAS AT HINDLEAP, SUSSEX

Dick Figlar's article is timely and fascinating, but I should like to start by discussing the differences between his climate and that in the south of England, as the USDA climate zones can be misleading when applied to the UK.

The South Carolina climate has more extremes than ours, the summer temperatures being reliably higher and those in winter sometimes significantly lower. The most important difference is that magnolias growing there have more chance of ripening their wood in summer, rendering them more able to cope with winter cold. The difference in the winter is also important, in that it is very rare for the temperature to remain below freezing there for more than 24 hours, so the soil never really freezes. In contrast, we sometimes have long periods when the temperature stays below zero. Magnolias hardy in S. Carolina therefore, may not be hardy in the UK. However, species which flower too early in S. Carolina may be later and less prone to damage in the UK.

Finally, when reading these notes, readers should remind themselves that there has not been a severe winter in the UK recently.

MAGNOLIA MAUDIAE

Planted 2003: slow growth to 2m. Like others I have seen in the UK appears a bit chlorotic. No frost damage. No flowers yet.

MAGNOLIA DIANICA (now M. LAEVIFOLIA)

Planted 2003: spreading growth to 1.8m. Perfectly hardy (it can be grown in Belgium where M. campbellii is tender). Flowered from the first spring, and covers itself with fragrant flowers every year now. A superb plant.

MAGNOLIA INSIGNIS

Two plants from AC554 collected in Yunnan at about 1700m in 1993. Vigorous upright growth to 4.5 and 6m. No frost damage on either. One flowers profusely, and has ivory flowers of a similar size to M. 'Nimbus' in June and July.

These have a distinctive scent and a most attractive dark boss of stamens. A superb summer flowering magnolia.

MAGNOLIA CONIFERA var. CHINGII

Planted 2005, Fastigiate growth to 2.5m. No frost damage, but no flowers yet.

MAGNOLIA FORDIANA and YUYUANENSIS

One, planted 2005 in a very sheltered position, had its terminal growth frosted out in the first winter, but has since recovered and is beginning to grow well. A plant labelled Manglietia yuyuanensis planted in 2006 has thrived and is growing well. No flowers yet.

MAGNOLIA LOTUNGENSIS

This was killed here in its first winter, but I am not sure the plant was true to name.

MAGNOLIA PLATYPETALA, CAVALERIEI and MOTO

I have not been able to obtain these species.

MAGNOLIA FOVEOLATA

This was purchased some time ago, but is not true to name.

M. ernestii, M. chapensis, M. crassipes (syn. Manglietia pachyphylla), M. skinneriana, M. lanuginosa, M. duclouxii, M. martinii, and hybrids of M. figo have all grown here for at least 3 winters without damage.

M. macclurei and M. figo have suffered frost damage, and I have serious doubts as to the survival of the former.

Finally M. doltsopa, grown from a Cornish seedling, does superbly, having grown well above the South wall on which it was planted. The top defoliates most winters in our gales, but the tree (now 8m high) flowers and sets fruit every year.

MIKE ROBINSON

GROWING EVERGREEN MAGNOLIAS IN NORTH DEVON

My garden is near the coast in Barnstaple and as a result has a favoured microclimate; tentatively at the equivalent of USDA Zone 9, although these zones do not transfer easily to the British Isles as the wood ripening is not as great due to the cooler summers. The compensation is a long growing season and mild winters here in the southwest at least.

I started out with section *Michelia* in 1991 when I obtained *Magnolia ernestii* (*Michelia wilsonii*) and planted it by a tall wall, not knowing how hardy it would be. It grew steadily and had to be pruned after ten years. It started producing disappointingly cream coloured flowers after about eight years, but it was only last year that there was definite yellow in the cream. I am hopeful that yellower forms will be selected.

Magnolia doltsopa and *M. nitida* followed in 1994, again near a wall where they have grown well, *M. doltsopa* producing a fine crop of wonderfully scented flowers in March, *M. nitida* has yet to flower.

Emboldened, in 2004 I planted seedlings of *Magnolia foveolata*, *M. laevifolia*, *M. martinii* and *M. maudiae* in the open and they have been fine, *M. laevifolia* has flowered well but is a poor form, and *M. maudiae* flowered for the first time last year in March. The rate of growth of the seedlings has been phenomenal except for *M. foveolata* var. *cinerascens*. *M. martinii* has won the height race at over 2m in three years! I notice there are flower buds for next year, and it seems very hardy here.

Albeit a hybrid, another magnolia I am fond of which was not mentioned in Dick's article, is *Magnolia* x *foggii*, two of the selected forms of which I grow. Quite vigorous growers, but ultimately not too large, I would think they would be good for a smaller garden. The flowers arise from velvet brown buds and have the good grace to drop off before turning brown. They are produced in succession, and flowering is over several weeks from April onwards. The photo of my 'Allspice' plant was taken on the First of May this year (2007).

I have planted many others over the last year or so – *Magnolia odora* (might be a bit tender),

MAGNOLIA x FOGGII 'Allspice'

JOHN MARSTON

M. lotungensis (untouched last winter), *M. yuyuanensis* (growing strongly with lovely red new growth), *M. macclurei* (somewhat tender) and *M. conifera* var. *chingii* (needed more moisture than I gave it first time round, but since replanted in a moister place). *M. foveolata* with russet all over has also been slow growing. Another plant of *M. ernestii* in the open is also growing away well. I have planted two more *M. laevifolia*, given to me by Maurice Foster and labelled unequivocally 'best form'. I have high hopes for these.

Maybe in another ten years there will have been enough time to analyse the performance of these recent introductions, and sort out the beautiful from the boring, and not only for flower but also for foliage where much of their appeal will lie.

JOHN MARSTON

NOTES ON THE 'NEW' EVERGREEN MAGNOLIAS IN WEST KENT

I must confess to having been a sceptic about the relative hardiness of the 'new' evergreen magnolias. Mostly at home at relatively low altitude in the benevolent climate of S China, they thrive for example in Yunnan and though with only 40in of rain annually, this normally falls between April and October. Winter is dry and mild. Small wonder that the capital Kunming is known as the 'City of Eternal Spring'.

It is difficult to replicate these conditions at 500ft in Kent with exposure to the north and east, a rainfall of 30in spread across the year, summers often dry, winters usually soggy or freezing, and with spring stuttering on, full of false promises.

Even so, my scepticism about hardiness has been questioned by Dick Figlar's experience. Although his climate in S Carolina, with contrasting hot summers and cold winters, could hardly be more different from ours and in theory should be even less suitable, to date his hardiness observations have been more than encouraging.

Having said that, I still have reservations about reliability in our own conditions, as the plants have not yet been properly tested in a 'real' winter. Over the last 15 years, our lowest temperature has been a brief –8°C and sooner or later we could experience a nasty shock.

Experience so far here in Kent has been limited and mixed. Our *Magnolia doltsopa*, 18 years from a cutting, has grown famously to over 11m and makes a superb, full-foliaged evergreen tree. Planted in a sheltered SW corner of the house, it now tops the roof. It flowers freely every year, the fragrant creamy white flowers wreathing the shoots from the leaf axils. It flowers a little too early and some swelling flower buds are occasionally lost to a March frost. It has twice been completely frosted. Curiously, flowers frosted in the bud seem to open normal size, but the colour of brown paper. Even with these negatives, we would not be without it.

Magnolia insignis has 3in ivory flowers stained reddish pink, which are solitary and borne in succession in summer. Though individually quite appealing, they do not colour a dense upright tree which has reached 7m in 15 years, but more brightly coloured forms exist. Wind - sheltered from N and E, the glossy lanceolate/narrowly ovate leaves make it one of our best large evergreens.

Six *Magnolia laevifolia* have been set out for 4 years in various positions and have all grown well. It is variable in foliage, flower, habit and bud velvet. It flowers in late spring and is so far bud hardy. The small leaves, rusty velvet buds and fragrant white flowers combine beautifully and are particularly good in the cultivar 'Velvet and Cream'. Low bushy forms make it ideal for the small garden as it is quite slow but flowers young. Gangly forms are readily espaliered. In favoured woodland conditions arborescent forms can make 4m plus.

Magnolia fordiana has been planted out for 4 years, but has not yet flowered. It is grafted onto *M. kobus* and has reached about 1.3m. It is hardy – there is a nice bushy plant in the Hillier Arboretum over 20 years old. *M. ernestii* has been in the garden for 4 years but also not yet flowered.

M. figo, out for 3 years, is slow and only 0.5m, but I have seen it elsewhere as a dense, small leaved bushy shrub. The flowers are cream stained purple, scattered, small and relatively insignificant, but intensely fragrant, smelling of bananas or lemon drop. 'Purple Queen' is a cultivar with rich blackish purple flowers. A plant for close appreciation.

For the rest, I have *M. maudiae*, *M. crassipes*, *M. skinneriana*, *M. compressa*, *M. duclouxii*, *M. macclurei* and *M. cathcartii* in the greenhouse on a starvation fitness regime, hardening them up in preparation for the rigours of the garden.

Finally, it is worth keeping an eye open for hybrids. Work has been going on in Australia and New Zealand using mostly *M. maudiae*, *M. figo*, *M. laevifolia* and *M. doltsopa* and there could be interesting results in both colour and hardiness.

MAURICE FOSTER

Rhododendron conservation at Nymans

ED IKIN

NYMANS HOLDS A NATIONALLY important collection of rhododendrons. Significant both for the large number of wild collected accessions and the quality of plants themselves, the collection is now under threat and we are taking urgent steps to ensure its future survival.

The Messel family, who owned Nymans, subscribed heavily to the expeditions of Ernest Wilson, Joseph Rock, Frank Kingdon Ward and George Forrest throughout the first half of the 20th century. Close friendships and rivalries with fellow Wealden gardeners drove much of their acquisition, and one-upmanship may have been responsible for some of the more spectacular taxa we now grow! Of particular note in the collection are *Rhododendron macabeanum* KW7724, *R. wardii* KW5736, *R. russatum* R11284, *R. sulfureum* F15782 and *R. morii* WILS10955. Nymans has shown rhododendrons for over a century and achieved many AGMs and 'Best in Shows' with its exhibits.

RHODODENDRON MACABEANUM KW7724 – widely regarded as one of the finest forms of this exceptional species   DAVID MASTERS

Traditionally, Nymans rhododendrons have enjoyed the conditions the garden offers. A fertile, freely draining, sandy loam soil, mild climate and ample tree cover allowed fragile taxa to establish quickly and thrive, and rhododendrons became the most significant element of the garden's plant collection. However, in more recent times, previously strong and healthy specimens have started to show a marked decline in their condition and this is linked to a number of factors.

The Great Storm of October 1987 had far-reaching effects for the ecology and micro-climate of Nymans Garden. Kent and Sussex took the brunt of a hurricane that blew on countryside waterlogged from heavy rain and with trees still in leaf. Rootplates of the biggest, most established trees were loosened in the saturated conditions and the damage to these heavily wooded counties was extraordinary. Nymans alone lost over 400 trees that night.

The initial shock to the garden was the sudden exposure of previously sheltered shrubs with 80% of the tree cover disappearing overnight. The mature canopy of trees that stood over Nymans always guided the planting of fragile understory shrubs and the shelter provided by sweet chestnut and oak was a factor in the successful establishment of sensitive or tender taxa. A second, less obvious influence of the storm was the effect of the clear up operation.

The storm created a level of damage that gardeners had simply never encountered. The National Trust, custodians of Nymans since 1953,

80% OF TREES WERE LOST at Nymans during the storm, including much of the canopy protecting rhododendrons

THE FLATTENED PINETUM, which took the brunt of the storm   © NATIONAL TRUST

compromised by having to work around established shrubs.

The second, less tangible factor is climate change. The headlines dwell on the apocalyptic nature of global warming but the reality for gardeners is winters without prolonged frost, torrential pulses of rain, extended periods of extreme heat and drought and unseasonably strong winds. Although it is unscientific to blame all our rhododendron's woes on climate change – our current conditions are very different to the Himalayan areas our plants were collected in. We have noticed rhododendrons suffering particularly during extended droughts and wet winters, especially where loss of tree cover has increased exposure. A decline in desirable conditions has increased susceptibility to *Phytophthora* and Honey Fungus. Whilst *P. ramorum* has yet to appear at Nymans, other pathogenic members of the genus are resulting in the characteristic 'wilting' appearance of established rhododendrons.

invested heavily to return its flagship gardens back to normality as quickly as possible – entailing the arrival of enormous agricultural and forestry plant and machinery. Whole trees were dragged out of delicate garden areas and stacks of tree stumps were buried in deep holes. With the benefit of hindsight, it is apparent that the post-storm clearance caused significant damage to the structure of some garden areas.

Nymans grows many of its best Kingdon Ward accessions in an area called 'Large-Leaved Rhododendron Shaw' and nearby 'School Copse' accommodates several tender taxa. These areas took some of the heaviest wear from the machinery used post-storm and the soil structure has fundamentally changed – being heavily waterlogged for large parts of the year with anaerobic conditions in the topsoil. New woody plants, such as the normally vigorous *Nothofagus* fail within 2–3 years of planting and many of the mature rhododendron species are declining in vigour. We aim to partially rectify this decline with deep decompaction of these areas – backfilling with expanded aggregate and organic matter to rebuild the damaged soil profile, although this work is inevitably

Although the state of our rhododendrons is worrying, we are aiming to both stabilise the current decline and create sufficient back-up stocks to ensure no taxa are lost to cultivation. Through the use of bracken compost and

RHODODENDRON ELEGANTULUM showing signs of *Phytophthora* infection   ED IKIN

beneficial mycorrhizal products such as Antagon, we maximise soil and plant health, allowing rhododendrons to fight pathogens and stress better. We find symbiotic products can stabilise plants displaying early symptoms of *Phytophthora* but can rarely pull plants 'back from the brink'. Antagon is applied as a base dressing around shrubs in mid-spring and lightly worked into the soil.

Conservation propagation is rarely straightforward; the minimal new growth that weak plants produce is rarely suitable for grafting or cuttings and micropropagation often the only option. We set up a 3 year programme to create back-up stock for all endangered taxa, some material being cut back in the first year to produce suitable growth – working with partner nurseries specialising in grafting and micropropagation. The level of co-operation and help we have received has been heartening with much of the work being done on a quid pro quo basis and we are now receiving back some of the first plants to be propagated.

Where we go next is an interesting debate – I do not believe we need to hang on to taxa if they will not grow happily at Nymans. I would be happy to see some of our propagated material go to gardens in Ireland or Scotland if they would grow better there. Extreme summers such as 2006 quickly identify taxa happy in a changed climate and as the National Trust needs to present magnificent gardens to its visitors, we must take care to grow plants that thrive with a minimum of intervention.

Ed Ikin

is Head Gardener at Nymans Garden, Sussex

Current taxonomy – *Rhododendron vanderbiltianum* MERR.

GEORGE ARGENT, MICHAEL MÖLLER & ALEXANDRA CLARK

RHODODENDRON VANDERBILTIANUM flowering in the wild

WILLEM DE WILDE

DURING A FIELD VISIT to Mt. Kemiri (Aceh Province) in Sumatra, the first author was excited to find a cream coloured rhododendron which was clearly not a *Vireya*. Only one non-vireya had previously been recorded from this area, which was *Rhododendron atjehense* Sleumer (subgenus *Hymenanthes* (Blume) K.Koch) This species was very much in evidence, flowering abundantly with its large, pale purple flowers. The smaller, cream flowered rhododendron was also common in the alpine shrubbery and it was at first thought that it must be a new species. It was somewhat chastening to see a plant of this same species without flowers which was immediately recognised as *R. vanderbiltianum* Merr., a species we had growing in the Royal Botanic Garden Edinburgh from a David Binney collection from the same mountain. This has never flowered for us in cultivation.

Rhododendron vanderbiltianum is a Sumatran endemic known only from a small group of mountains in the Losir area of Aceh Province: Mt. Losir; Mt. Goh Lembuh; Mt. Kemiri and Pang-mog.

Professor Sleumer in his *Flora Malesiana* account of *Rhododendron* (Sleumer 1966) included *R. vanderbiltianum* in his section *Pseudovireya* without any comment on its taxonomic position or relationships, despite the fact that it was illustrated in this account with large, widely open, funnel-shaped flowers, clearly unlike any of the other species in this section. From a morphological point of view it was the stamen arrangement which most immediately demonstrated that this species was not a *Vireya*. The stamens were of variable lengths, spread in an arc in the manner of an upturned grass rake, a common arrangement amongst non-vireya rhododendrons but quite unlike anything known in the vireyas. It also has vegetative buds fringed with simple hairs which would again be novel in a *Vireya*. Examination of herbarium specimens with fruits also confirmed that the seeds were without the tails characteristic of vireyas. In fact Merrill, following his original description of *R. vanderbiltianum*, clearly indicated that he did not think it a *Vireya* as he said: (Merrill 1940), *"perhaps allied to* R. leucobotrys *Ridl. of the Malay Peninsula"* (now a synonym of *R. moulmainense* Hook. f.) [Subg. *Azaleastrum* sect. *Choniastrum*]. An interesting observation and also possible further indication of its lack of relationship to *Vireya* was the fact that *R. vanderbiltianum* was heavily infested with the parasite *Exocarpos* (Santalaceae) but, despite extensive searching in the alpine shrubberies, this was never found on the associated *Vireya* species. If its position in *Pseudovireya* was correct, *R. adinophyllum* Merr. (another species of Section *Pseudovireya* endemic to the area) at least might also have been expected to be parasitized by this mistletoe-like plant.

Molecular phylogenetic procedures followed Sinclair *et al.* (2002) for internal transcribed spacer sequences of nuclear ribosomal DNA. The maximum parsimony placed *R. vanderbiltianum* on a polytomy (unresolved

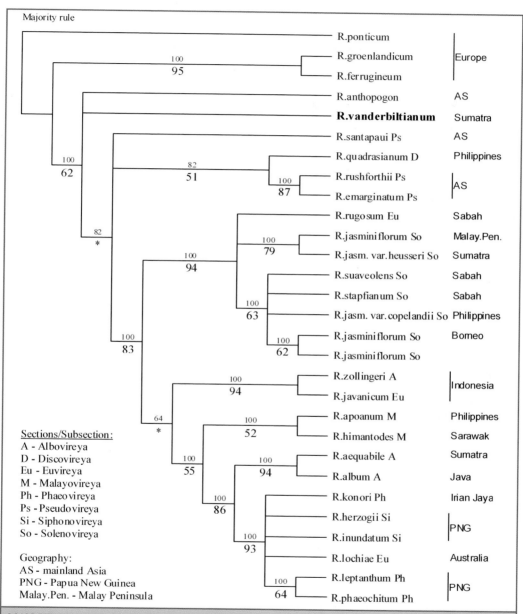

MAJORITY RULE CONSENSUS CLADOGRAM of 11 most parsimonious trees of 103 steps, CI=0.8738, RI=0.9297 and RC=0.8124, based on sequences of the nuclear ribosomal DNA internal transcribed spacer region, including the 5.8S gene. Numbers above branches are branch frequencies, numbers below are bootstrap values of 10000 replicates of random addition with TBR on, MULTREES off. * denotes branches with <50% support.

RHODODENDRON VANDERBILTIANUM
with the parasite *Exocarpos*

GEORGE ARGENT

relationship) close to *R. anthopogon* D. Don [Subgenus *Rhododendron* sect. *Pogonanthum*] and outside the clade including taxa of Subgenus *Vireya* (see cladogram). This confirms Merrill's view that *R. vanderbiltianum*

is not a *Vireya*, although further work is needed to establish its precise relationships. Morphologically it is very similar to *R. crenulatum* Hutchinson ex Sleumer [Subgenus *Rhododendron* sect. *Maddenia*] from Laos and now reported from Vietnam (Rushforth 2007). Further investigation may link these species more closely.

In cultivation, *R. vanderbiltianum* has proved to be very difficult, as Rushforth (2007) reported for *R. crenulatum*. In the RBGE, *R. vanderbiltianum* grows slowly and has never flowered. Most of the plants from two different collections have died. This is puzzling as *R. adinophyllum* and *R. sumatranum* Merr. both grow and flower freely in cultivation and grow alongside *R. vanderbiltianum* on Mt. Kemiri. This is a great pity as the plants are most attractive in the wild.

ACKNOWLEDGEMENTS

We thank Dr David Chamberlain for helpful comments, the Royal Botanic Garden Edinburgh for supporting the field and laboratory work and Dr W de Wilde for the use of his photograph of *R. vanderbiltianum* taken in the wild.

George Argent
is a research associate at RBGE with a special interest in SE Asian flora.

Michael Möller
is DNA analyst/ cytologist at RBGE with a special interest in the Gesneriaceae.

Alexandra Clark
is a research scientist developing molecular techniques for biodiversity research and running the genetic analysis systems.

References ■ Merrill, ED (1940). Botanical results of the George Vanderbilt Sumatran expedition 1939. Plants from Mt. *Löser. Notulae Naturae*, The Academy of Natural Sciences of Philadelphia 47: 1–9. Rushforth, K (2007). Vietnamese Rhododendrons in Cultivation in the UK. *Rhododendron Species* (Rhododendron Species Foundation Yearbook #2) 71–77. Sinclair, W T, Mill, RR, Gardner, MF, Woltz, P, Jaffré, T, Preston, J, Hollingsworth, ML, Ponge, A and Möller, M (2002). Evolutionary relationships of the New Caledonian heterotrophic conifer, *Parasitaxus usta* (Podocarpaceae), inferred from chloroplast *trn*L-F intron / spacer and nuclear rDNA ITS2 sequences. *Plant Systematics and Evolution* 233(1–2): 79–104. Sleumer H (1966). Rhododendron, in *Flora Malesiana* Series I, 6: 474–668. Groningen, The Netherlands.

Children of Chance – breeding camellias

NICK CREEK

A DELIGHTFUL MIX of 'Browncreek's' and other camellias (*see next page for varieties*)   NICK CREEK

I HAVE BEEN INVOLVED with plants since leaving school in the early 1970s and spent the first 20 years of my working life growing orchids at the nurseries at Stonehurst, a private estate, which at that time had one of the leading horticultural nurseries in the country. Here I was able to gain the very valuable experience of producing hundreds of hybrids over those years, many becoming award-winning plants for the nursery at RHS Orchid Shows.

Things changed after the Great Storm of 1987, before which Stonehurst had two separate nurseries, the other being a general shrub nursery, growing a wide range of trees and shrubs. After the storm many staff retired or left at the owner's request, but because it had escaped with only minor damage, the orchid nursery was asked to absorb the sales of 'Stonehurst' shrubs including camellias and rhododendrons. Over the next few years the shrub stocks were sold off and not replaced and

by the early 1990s Mr. Strauss, the owner, asked me to take over the production and showing of his camellia collection which had earned a very high reputation in the past.

I had no formal training in taking cuttings or any other methods of increasing these plants and the first few years saw many mishaps – including the near loss of an entire batch of camellia cuttings due to faulty soil heating cables failing when the beds were full with new cuttings, taken just two weeks before. Needless to say, only the stronger *Camellia japonica* varieties rooted, unlike the x *williamsii* hybrids which did not!

With a wish to enlarge the collection, I set about starting a breeding programme.

The first year's seed was only taken from those varieties which had yielded the most pods, all of which were open-pollinated by the many bees present. Since that time I have made a number of hand-crosses using the most fertile of parents, as well as continuing to take pods from open-pollinated plants. 'Chance' has played an important role in my breeding. It took nearly five years of patience before the first seedling flowered and was it worth the wait? Yes! Yes! It really was worth the wait! 'It' being an open-pollinated seedling from *C. x williamsii* 'Mary Jobson', with a much larger bloom of rich, deep phlox pink and semi-double. The growth habit may be more open than its parent, but not all plants need to be grown into an upright bush. This new variety lends itself to being trained against a wall or fence and is appropriately named *C.* 'Browncreek's Delight'.

Regarding the process of raising new seedlings: most seed pods ripen from late September onwards. After collecting the year's labours in the autumn, once the first pods split, it is wise to sow them as soon as possible. This is best done by using pure sphagnum moss which I have found is the ideal medium. Delaying this process will increase the failure rate of germination as the seed tends to dry out over time. Using seed from the same crossing or, if open-pollinated, the same parent, I use a small pot or plastic freezer bag. I squeeze most of the moisture out of the moss and place up to 10 fresh seeds per container on a layer of moss. This is covered with another layer of moss and placed in a warm dark position – around 15–21°C. After 6–8 weeks they are checked for any sign of germination. If they have germinated they can be transferred into pots containing equal parts leaf mould and garden compost and moved into the cold frame, greenhouse or, in my case, the spare room. It is at this time that new seedlings are at most risk – not from damping off but from four-legged furry friends or fiends – MICE! In one night these little blighters can destroy your entire year's work, as I found out much to my dismay early on in my attempts. Camellia seeds contain a rich supply of oils which they enjoy, so make sure that your seedlings are well protected against them. I found that covering them with 5mm wire mesh helps or, as is my practice, keeping the entire year's harvest in the spare room, at least until the first of the proper leaves have formed, makes a world of difference.

From now on keeping the seedlings on the move will reap huge rewards. The quicker they grow on, the faster any special new varieties emerge. Once they have outgrown the first sized pot, I use a growing medium of 75% peat or similar medium, 20%

chipped bark, 5% grit and a trace of slow release fertilizer and dolomite lime. Within the first 5 years of sowing you should have bloomed a number of those seedlings, and maybe one or two that have improved in shape or colour from their parents. If you are unlucky, some may take the next 10–15 years to flower although it is said that the better blooms will come from those seedlings which flower later on. But who can tell?

As to the best varieties I have used within *C. x williamsii*, the most prolific has been *C.* 'Mary Jobson' by far. Others, including *C.* 'Elizabeth de Rothschild', 'J.C. Williams', 'Philippa Forward' and 'Golden Spangles' have been rewarding as well, some even producing white blooms. Occasionally seeds have come from varieties

CAMELLIA VARIETIES IN BOWL DISPLAY
1. *C. japonica* 'Dr. Tinsley'
2. *C. x williamsii* 'Browncreek's Phoenix'
3. *C. japonica* 'Mrs Mac'
4. *C. japonica* 'Browncreek's Butterfly'
5. *C. x williamsii* 'Browncreek's Destiny'
6. *C. x williamsii* 'Browncreek's Melody'
7. *C. x williamsii* 'Mary Jobson'
8. *C. x williamsii* 'Daintiness'
9. *C. japonica* 'Elizabeth Rose Open'
10. *C. japonica* 'Browncreek's Pixie'
11. *C. japonica* 'Browncreek's Midget'
12. *C. japonica* 'Browncreek's Damask'
13. *C. x williamsii* 'Browncreek's Sunset'
14. *C. japonica* 'Browncreek's Butterfly'
15. *C. japonica* 'Billie McCaskill'
16. *C. japonica* 'Hagaromo'
17. *C. japonica* 'Browncreek's Opal'
18. *C. japonica* 'Browncreek's Passion'
19. *C. japonica* 'Browncreek's Diadem'
20. *C. japonica* 'Browncreek's Harlequin'

such as C. 'Daintiness' and 'Jury's Yellow'. Of these rare crosses, three fine seedlings have since flowered from 'Daintiness'. The first came from a cross using pollen from *C. japonica* 'Rogetsu' and this I have named *C.* 'Browncreek's Purity', due to the large pure white semi-double blooms. The second, a cross with *C. japonica* 'Wildfire' has given me large deep red formal double blooms and this I have named *C.* 'Browncreek's Carmen', its habit is upright and bushy. Finally, and the latest to bloom, is *C.* 'Browncreek's Sweetness', a semi-double like *C.* 'Daintiness', but a brighter, clear pink in colour. As of now only two seedlings from *C.* 'Jury's Yellow' have bloomed, one a single to semi-double pure white called *C.* 'Browncreek's Sunrise'. However, the best by far is *C.* 'Browncreek's Sunset', similar in size and shape to Jury's Yellow, but of a rich bright red colour overall, stronger in growth and much more bushy. Both these seedlings are the result of using pollen from *C. japonica* 'Sylva'.

Amongst the *Camellia japonica* seedlings, the variety has been less exciting, but a number of single flowered offspring, three of which have bloomed from chance pollinations of *C.* 'Clarissa' are worth mention. *C.* 'Browncreek's Twilight' was first, being a blush pink, followed by *C.* 'Browncreek's Moonbeam', a large pure white and finally *C.* 'Browncreek's Chiffon' a very large delightful soft pale pink having an upright bushy growth habit.

The most surprising parent of all was the much maligned *C.* 'Beni Hassaku' which is a slow, compact, bushy grower of a single rose pink colour with only 5 petals. A prolific seed producer, the range of colours has been from pure white through every shade of pink to almost red. The best seedlings from this parent are *C.* 'Browncreek's Gem', a pure white semi-double bloom on a neat compact, upright bush, *C.* 'Browncreek's Pageantry' with large soft pink semi-double to loose peony shaped blooms and more recently, a large blush pink single called *C.* 'Browncreek's Lustre'. An unusual coloured coral pink anemone shaped seedling from a cross of *C.* 'Mattie Cole' with *C.* 'Coral Queen' has a primrose yellow mass of petaloids in the centre. It is like its mother – low growing and bushy in habit and, with a break from my usual way of naming my own seedlings, it has been

called 'Buffy's Beauty' after one of our old Bantam hens that we allowed to wander around the garden some time past. It flowers early to mid season. Another, more recent seedling of *C.* 'Mattie Cole', named *C.* 'Browncreek's Harlequin' is the mating of pollen from the semi-double variety *C.* 'Robert Strauss', again similar in growth habit to *C.* 'Mattie Cole'. It is a semi-double pale pink, striped with light red markings, with a central mass of rabbit eared petaloids giving it the look of an anemone formed bloom, usually flowering mid season.

Finally, waiting in the pipeline I have a range of mixed seedlings from *C.* 'Salutation' and a number of *C. sasanqua* varieties growing on for the future. Within these hybrids there should hopefully be some exciting colour breaks. Maybe white flowers, with luck, in the *C. reticulata* bloodline.

Six years ago Stonehurst Nurseries closed and I now work at Imberhorne Lane Nursery in East Grinstead, West Sussex. I am still raising new camellia seedlings and I hope within the next year or so that many of these will be available for sale at the nursery.

I am still showing regularly and continue to enjoy success. During the last three or four years I have exhibited my new seedlings at the RHS Early and Main Camellia Shows at Vincent Square in London where single blooms are displayed and judged against each other within the classes given and my varieties have been awarded a number of First and Second prizes.

As to the name – Browncreek – it is simply a combination of my own and my partner's surnames – Brown and Creek!

Having plenty of patience will, in time, give you the reward of seeing your first flower-bud opening. This is justly satisfying and with luck on your side it will mature over the next year or so into a new variety that supersedes its parents in colour, shape or vigour. Hopefully, after reading this, you will be encouraged to try your hand and grow your own seedlings in future. Good luck!

Nick Creek

is Horticulturist & Camellia Expert at Imberhorne Lane Nursery in West Sussex

Warren Berg – a personal tribute

STEVE HOOTMAN

WARREN BERG in a *Rhododendron hodgsonii* tree in Bhutan, 1988

WITH THE PASSING OF WARREN BERG in 2006, the rhododendron world has lost a most significant figure, and surely one of its finest ambassadors. His collection of species rhododendrons was unmatched in North America, with the exception only of the Rhododendron Species Foundation (RSF) and, possibly, the collection of his long-time friend and fellow species aficionado, June Sinclair, who still maintains her garden on the water's edge in the mild climate of Puget Sound, just a few miles from the Berg garden. But not only was Warren considered, in North America and internationally, to be among the foremost experts on species rhododendrons, he was also a noted rhododendron hybridizer. His primary garden on the shore of the Hood Canal off Puget Sound of Washington State was famous for its collection of rare species in combination with outstanding specimens of his own hybrids. Many of the plants in Warren's garden became almost as well-known as the man himself. His superb and perfectly grown large specimens of *Rhododendron proteoides* and *R. pronum* for example, were not only unique in North America, but possibly the finest examples of their kind in cultivation anywhere.

For example, his best *R. pronum* was so large that although we took 50 to 60 cuttings from it every summer for propagation at the RSF, you would never know from looking at the plant that anything was missing.

Warren first became interested in rhododendrons over 40 years ago while living just south of Seattle. In the 1970s he moved to the much milder climate along the Hood Canal, west of Seattle. In this garden, he was able to grow fine specimens of many species that are considered a bit tender in most of the Pacific Northwest. Species such as *R. macabeanum, sinogrande, mallotum, edgeworthii, arboreum* ssp. *zeylanicum* and even the rare *R. subansiriense* flourished in his sheltered garden. It was about this time that he became involved with the Rhododendron Species Foundation, then still a young organization. From that point until his death, Warren was a prominent and active participant in virtually every aspect of the functioning of the RSF. In addition to serving for many years and in many positions on the Board of Directors, he was integral in establishing several sections of the original garden plantings. Many of the plants now accessioned and growing

A FINE SPECIMEN of *Rhododendron pronum* in Warren's garden   WARREN BERG

A SMALL SECTION of Warren's beautifully maintained garden, featuring *Rhododendron proteoides*   WARREN BERG

fact, it was Mr Wada who provided Warren with one of his best known introductions into North America – the dwarf form of *R. keiskei* that eventually became known as 'Yaku Fairy', a plant that Warren and many others would use extensively in their hybridizing programs.

Warren began hybridizing almost from the beginning of his interest in rhododendrons with many of his early hybrids ending up in the gardens of friends and neighbors. As he developed a better eye for a good plant and his collection continued to improve with clones such as 'Yaku Fairy', his hybrid crosses also improved. Some of his best efforts were with the smaller growing and dwarf lepidote species and hybrids. Similar to the very successful 'bird' series of dwarf lepidote hybrids that have been produced by the Cox family at Glendoick, Warren had great success with these small-scale but floriferous species and hybrids. He was very careful about naming and distributing his hybrids, preferring to trial, evaluate and grow the selections for many years before releasing them into the trade. It often took the prompting of his friends and fellow rhododendron growers to register and name a clone that was well known to be of exceptional quality. For example, June Sinclair described the then newly registered *R.* 'June Bee' as "*a very good white with excellent*

in the RSF collection were either donated by or obtained as cuttings from Warren, who, in addition to his own early collections in Japan, Korea and elsewhere, had been collecting outstanding forms of species for many years. Remarkably, of the approximately 11,000 total accessions in the RSF collection, close to 900 came directly from Warren, either as plants or cuttings. Indeed, until the year of his death, I made regular visits to his garden to 'fill in the gaps' for the RSF, as it were, collecting cuttings and accepting fine specimens grown from his own wild seed.

Like most collectors of rare or unusual plants, Warren's plants came from a wide variety of sources. Most of his early species material was acquired from friends and gardens in the United Kingdom and elsewhere in Europe. In later years, Warren's collection and garden became much more comprehensive as he was able to feature specimens of rare species grown from seed that he or others had collected in the wild.

In his professional life, Warren was a pilot for Northwest Airlines (among other things, he flew 747 jets to Europe, Japan and Korea). On his regular flights to Japan, Warren had ample opportunity to visit local nurseries and to develop friendships with rhododendron collectors and nurserymen in that country. He became friends with both Hideo Suzuki and Koichiro Wada, and spent a great deal of time with both of these well-known and respected horticulturists. In

RHODODENDRON PACHYSANTHUM 'Pachy Bee', a fine selection grown and named by Warren from seed sent to him by Peter Cox   WARREN BERG

RHODODENDRON 'JUNE BEE', named in honour of his great friend, June Sinclair   WARREN BERG

RHODODENDRON 'GOLFER', one of Warren's hybrids, named in honour of his wife Pat who was an avid fan of the sport   WARREN BERG

foliage, very adaptable and an extremely easy doer. Like all of Warren's hybrids it had a long trial period before he named and registered it. It took years of pressure from fans of the plant before this clone was chosen for its superior qualities." Warren responded to her praise with "Some of that pressure, as you might know, was from June, so rather than get shot, I named it for her." Most of the registered Berg hybrids bear the epithet 'Bee' in their name. Many of these hybrids are still widely propagated, marketed and grown including such famous cultivars as R. 'Patty Bee', 'Ginny Gee', 'Golfer' 'Wee Bee' and 'Too Bee' among many others.

As he became more interested in the wild species, Warren utilized his contacts both in the USA and Japan to organize botanical excursions into the mountains of Japan, making his first collecting trips in the early 1970s. Many of the plants collected on these trips eventually found their way into the RSF where they formed the core of the early collection, as did the selected forms of various azaleas and other species that Warren had collected from nurseries in his forays throughout Japan.

In the mid 1970s, Warren extended his explorations to the then independent Himalayan kingdom of Sikkim and Cheju Island, Korea. In Sikkim, Warren was one of a group of over two dozen members of the American Rhododendron Society visiting the country under the leadership of Britt and Jean Smith of Kent, Washington. This was the first organized tour of Sikkim by any group from the USA. The seed of those classic Himalayan species collected on this trip provided a welcome and major boost to the availability of true species in cultivation. Outstanding forms of *Rhododendron* species such as *R. cinnabarinum*, *griffithianum*, *grande*, *thomsonii*, *arboreum*, *argipeplum* and many others grown from this seed can still to be found growing in the RSF and in countless private collections in North America.

With the help of his friend Hideo Suzuki, Warren arranged an exploration of Cheju Island off the southern coast of Korea where he collected three species on the slopes of the dormant volcano Mt. Halla, at 6,400ft. (1,950m), the highest point on the island. In addition to the azaleas *R. weyrichii* and *yedoense* var. *poukhanense*, Warren collected seed and plants of the dwarf form of the deciduous species *R. mucronulatum*

RHODODENDRON 'WEE BEE', another fine dwarf hybrid from Warren ('Patricia' x *keiskei* 'Yaku Fairy')   WARREN BERG

which covered the upper slopes and rim of the crater. This taxon is now known as var. *chejuense* or var. *taquetii*. Warren selected and collected several particularly dwarf forms with exceptionally colored flowers. The plant that he considered the finest was named 'Crater's Edge' and this selection remains one of Warren's most popular and widely grown introductions.

In 1983, just a few years after China 'opened up' for those of us from the West; Warren was finally able to explore the famous and floristically rich mountains through which Rock, Kingdon Ward, Forrest and many others had trekked decades earlier. The first of Warren's many journeys to the Sino-Himalaya was to explore the Mt. Sigunian range in western Sichuan. On this, and all of his subsequent trips to this region, he was always on the lookout for species such as *R. bureavioides, roxieanum, phaeochrysum* and the like, understanding the need for interesting foliage throughout the year.

Warren led a group of Americans to southeastern Tibet in 1986 in an attempt to cross the fabled Doshong La. The deep snow prevented his group from reaching the pass but they were able to explore the nearby passes Sirge La and Temo La where they made many collections, including *R. wardii, faucium, principis, uvariifolium* and *cerasinum* among others. On their return to Chengdu, a brief stop in the Wolong Panda Reserve allowed for the collection of species such as *R. augustinii*, and *balangense*, then still unknown in the west. There are dozens of now quite large and mature specimens of numerous species in the RSF collection grown from seed collected on this trip. He was almost certainly one of the first westerners in the modern era to visit this remote part of the Himalaya.

In 1988, Warren returned to the Himalaya, joining Keith Rushforth, Peter Cox, Ted and Romy Millais, and several others in an exploration of the Kingdom of Bhutan. Numerous exciting species were found on this trip, including *R. flinckii, bhutanense, kesangiae* and the still rather mysterious taxon known as *R. hodgsonii* affinity.

Following his two trips to the high Himalaya, Warren focused his efforts in the high mountains of Sichuan and Yunnan Provinces, China and over the next several years, he explored regions

A BEAUTIFULLY GROWN *Rhododendron proteoides* in the Berg garden   WARREN BERG

such as the Cang Shan, 99 Dragons Pool, Beima Shan and the Mekong/Salween Divide in Yunnan. In Sichuan, he visited Gongga Shan, Erlang Shan, Zheduo Shan and Muli among others. Warren's favorite species was definitely the dwarf *R. proteoides*. It is the epitome of a 'collector's plant' and Warren was always very proud (in a humble fashion of course) of his best garden specimen. It is a species that he used extensively in his hybridizing ventures, especially in his later years, producing many fine dwarf hybrids with exceptional foliage interest. Although he had fine examples of this plant in his garden he always yearned to find it in the wild. This quest to find *R. proteoides* became the focus of every trip to China taken by Warren. Unfortunately, he was never able to find this species in the wild.

As he continued to participate in and lead expeditions to Asia, Warren gained a well-deserved reputation as a rhododendron species expert. His reputation as an intrepid, well-prepared and knowledge-able explorer was comple-mented and even high-lighted by his gregarious personality and personal charm. Through his writing, wonderful photographs, good humor and sharing nature, Warren Berg became the finest spokesman for rhododendrons in North America.

Steve Hootman

is Curator and Co-Executive Director of the Rhododendron Species Foundation, Washington

Book review

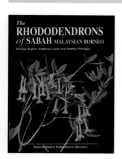

The Rhododendrons of Sabah, Malaysian Borneo
GEORGE ARGENT, ANTHONY LAMB & ANTHEA PHILLIPPS
Natural History Publications (Borneo) in association with
Royal Botanic Garden Edinburgh 2007

ISBN 983-812-111-8 25.5cm x 18.5cm Hardcover 280pp. US$69

Reviewed by Chris Callard
www.vireya.net

The original incarnation of this book appeared in 1988 as a modest, pocket-sized, softcover volume published by the Sabah Parks Trustees; one of a series of titles primarily aimed at visitors to the various parks situated within this Malaysian state on the island of Borneo. For many years it remained an elusive title to obtain in the West, although much sought after by the vireya-growing community and highly prized by those fortunate enough to secure a copy.

After nearly 20 years, *Rhododendrons of Sabah* has been re-born in full quarto hardcover glory; a revised, expanded and updated work providing the reader with a comprehensive account of the vireya rhododendrons of the region.

In the opening 'Introduction' the authors define *Rhododendron*, and in particular subgenus Vireya, and the distinctive traits of its members found in Sabah. Principally, these include the four types of scales found on the leaves, together with differences in the floral bracts, characters used in the identification and morphological classification of all vireyas.

The following chapter describes the different habitat types seen in Sabah, largely determined by increasing altitude, and discusses how the rhododendrons fit in to each type. This is expanded upon in the next chapter which examines the distribution of rhododendrons across Sabah, in particular along the main mountain ranges, graphically represented by four useful transect diagrams, as well as dealing with the issue of conservation.

Readers are then presented with a 'Key to the Flowering Rhododendrons of the Main Kinabalu Massif' – the most readily accessible place for those wishing to see vireyas in their natural environment. This covers the 26 species found on the mountain, including four species endemic to Kinabalu, and is followed by a complete 'Key to Sabah Rhododendrons' to enable identification of all 42 species found within the state (up, incidentally, from 35 species described in the 1988 edition).

The largest chapter in the book, at around two-thirds of the total page count, is devoted to botanical descriptions of each of the 42 Sabahan species, and follows the revision published by Dr. Argent last year – *Rhododendrons of Subgenus Vireya* (Royal Horticultural Society, London, 2006). Whilst the morphological data are, naturally, largely the same as those recorded in the earlier work, the reader will find a wealth of supplementary information, much specific to the location in which each species is found: habitat zone, microclimate, soil type, known pollinators, natural hybrids and more. All named natural hybrids are also represented along with a selection of a few of the more interesting un-named hybrids that have been found in the wild.

The book concludes with a comprehensive glossary of terms used, helpful line drawings of leaf and flower types, and several pages of fascinating scanning electron micrographs depicting scale types.

Perhaps one of the most immediately striking features of this book is the number of photographs accompanying the text; be they close-up images of flowers or foliage, plants growing in the wild or examples of habitat type, almost all are of excellent quality and of sufficiently good size to be of value to the reader. In addition, we are treated to a glorious selection of botanical illustrations, many reproduced full-page, painted by such celebrated artists as Rodella Purves and Eve Bennett. Many of the species descriptions are also enhanced with cameo portraits of the person responsible for discovering or introducing the plant.

In summary, there is much to commend this book and in many respects it combines the best of both worlds – not only is it an indispensable reference resource providing a scientific account of the rhododendrons but also, with so many photographs and illustrations, it holds the glamour of a 'coffee table' publication. In either guise, the reader will without doubt regularly return to this book. This reviewer's only gripe – it would have been an ideal opportunity to expand the content to encompass the states of Sarawak and Kalimantan, thereby including the remaining 13 species of the 55 to be found across the whole of Borneo.

Exceptional Plants 2007

Shows

VINCENT SQUARE

The 2007 spring camellia season was marked by highly variable weather conditions with many gardens reporting an early season and others a very late one. Both Vincent Square shows were badly affected by the weather, with the main show suffering from northerly winds and mostly cold conditions preceding it. The size of blooms was reduced by these unfavourable weather conditions which particularly impacted on the japonicas. The following camellias were of particular interest or excelled in this year's competitions.

Camellia transnokoensis
JENNIFER TREHANE

Camellia transnokoensis Hayata 1919 is a Taiwanese species of fairly recent introduction. It has small scented white flowers often with pink markings, and small leaves. The beauty is that that the flowers open all the way up the stem and the young growth is red or deep pink. The plant throws upright shoots which bear flowers the following year, and contributes to the garden landscape throughout the year.

Camellia **'Spring Festival'** (*C. cuspidata* x unknown) was raised by Toichi Domoto in California in 1976. It has a very neat, upright – almost columnar – habit with smallish leaves, and covers itself with small rose form pink flowers in mid-season. It is an unusual and outstanding plant which lends itself to formal planting on the smaller scale.

Camellia 'Pink Dahlia'
MICHAEL SHUTTLEWORTH

Camellia **'Pink Dahlia'** This truly different camellia was originated at the Kramer Brother nursery in California. The medium size blooms are a vivid almost shocking pink but their key characteristic is form rather than colour, unlike any other camellia the petals are highly ruffled appearing to be semi-double and on occasion almost formal-double giving them the appearance of a dahlia or even a very large cactus flower. Although listed as '*C. saluenensis* hybrid chance seedling' this magnificent plant does have two unfortunate characteristics. Firstly the new growth is regularly badly burnt on hot days giving the foliage the appearance of peach leaf curl, secondly, and possibly related, is the difficulty in establishing young plants.

Camellia **'Nuccio's Ruby'** A chance seedling of *C. reticulata* has yielded the very darkest of reticulata blooms, large to very large semi-double with ruffled petals. Normally these blooms have one significant problem in that the petals tend to be

Camellia 'Nuccio's Ruby'
MICHAEL SHUTTLEWORTH

thin and papery and consequently suffer badly from folding and other damage. Having said that the blooms exhibited at Vincent Square by David Davis of Warwickshire are the best examples I have ever seen both last year and this. These blooms showed good substance whilst maintaining both size and, most importantly, colour. I have now changed my opinion of this plant and strongly recommend it to those interested in *C. reticulata*.

Camellia **'Deep Scarlet'** Although labelled 'Deep Scarlet' this name is unregistered and the plant in question is almost certainly *Camellia* 'Deep Secret', a seedling of 'Scarlet Buoy' × 'Bob Hope'. The growth habit is upright and of medium density and rapidity. The flower is semi-double, cardinal red, veined even darker, and the anthers are lemon yellow on yellow filaments. The petals are remarkably uniform and even giving an almost artificial appearance to the blooms. The plant is readily available in commerce and should undoubtedly be grown widely.

Camellia 'Deep Secret'
JENNIFER TREHANE

Camellia **'Nuccio's Carousel'** has become the archetypal American-derived show camellia with the regular quality of the blooms never ceasing to surprise. Large to very large blooms, semi-double like overgrown shuttlecocks in pastel pink and cream. If I had to recommend one camellia to someone just starting out on the show bench, this might well be that plant. The uniformity of the flower is often amazing with a group of three or four cut blooms being indistinguishable between them. As an example of this plant's quality, I was recently accused of cheating by entering it in a competition because "it inevitably wins best in show". A sure fire winner.

Camellia 'Nuccio's Carousel'
MICHAEL SHUTTLEWORTH

ROSEMOOR

The date of the Rosemoor competition was perfect for an excellent display of the Loderi Group forms. This knocked on the head the common perception that Loderi are just 'big and blowsy', and of little subtlety. The perfect, tight and almost spherical trusses were a delight to behold and the scent was all-pervasive. Loderi Group should be present in all but the smallest collections (it can be pruned!). *R.* Loderi 'King George' is most commonly grown, but the best on this display was Colin Brown's ***R.* Loderi 'Pink Diamond'** — a worthy winner celebrating its centenary year.

R. **'Lady Digby'** (*facetum* × *strigillosum*) AM 1946 raised at Minterne and shown by Pam Hayward combines the elegance and fine truss of *R. strigillosum* with the later flowering of *R. facetum*, and is more sun tolerant than either. It is an excellent substitute for those species in cooler gardens or when midseason flowering is desired. All *R. strigillosum* hybrids seem

R. Loderi 'Pink Diamond'
TIMOTHY SWAN

to be good, but this one has been neglected recently in favour of *R*. 'Taurus' (*strigillosum* x 'Jean Marie de Montague'). *R*. 'Lady Digby' has the better foliage by far: the influence of *R. strigillosum* is much more apparent in the plant as a whole.

R. **'Douggie Betteridge'** (*fortunei* x 'Jalisco') AM 1986 raised by Edmund de Rothschild before 1970 is another contribution to Exbury's long success with *R. fortunei* hybrids. This one has good rounded foliage, and a 7-lobed corolla with very subtle colouring in shades of pink and cream. With better foliage than the Fred Wyniatt Group it so far seems more resistant to mildew than some of the Naomi Group.

R. 'Lady Digby'
GEORGE HARGREAVES

The presence of an unregistered hybrid of *Rhododendron sinogrande* (**R. 'Lord Rudolph'**) reminded us of the hidden treasures still to emerge from Caerhays. It is almost identical to the species, but the corolla, though yellow, also has nice shades of pink.

Of especial interest to the species connoisseur was a truss of a white flowered rhododendron from Barry Starling. Even the experts were uncertain as to which subsection it belonged – Irrorata or Maculifera being suggested. Raised from seed collected by Keith Rushforth (KR198) from Mt Omei, Sichuan in 1980, the plant has been flowering freely every year for over 10 years and has formed a dense shrub 2.5m x 2.5m with oblong-obovate leaves 15cm long x 5cm wide. The crimson-throated blooms form a 12-flowered truss with deep red pedicels. KR198 is listed as *R. pachytrichum* or a natural hybrid of *R. pachytrichum* and *R. strigillosum*. However, this unique plant is unlike either and must be propagated.

R. 'Douggie Betteridge'
GEORGE HARGREAVES

R. 'Lord Rudolph'
GEORGE HARGREAVES

Barry Starling's unidentified rhododendron species
GEORGE HARGREAVES

There was a splendid display of magnolias, with perhaps more yellows in one place than has been seen before. *M.* **'Lois'** is becoming well known as a true yellow with flowers opening before the emergence of the leaves. A superb plant with only one disadvantage – following its *M. acuminata* parent, it will eventually form a large tree: but magnolias respond well to pruning.

M. **'Daphne'** also stood out as something special. Nicely held and poised at the ends of branches in full foliage, the flowers stand out both on the show bench and in the landscape.

M. 'Lois'
GEORGE HARGREAVES

M. 'Daphne'
PHILIPPE DE SPOELBERCH

Tours

FOTA GARDENS, CORK, EIRE
Magnolia **'Charles Coates'**
(*sieboldii* x *tripetala*)
PREFERRED SITUATION: Semi-shade; fertile, moist and permeable soil that is acidic (needs peat); protect from strong winds.

This open-pollinated hybrid was named after the propagator who found it growing in the Azalea Garden at the Royal Botanic Gardens at Kew, in 1946. It grows rapidly when young to form a dense, rounded small tree with strongly upright stems and broad-spreading branches. This deciduous magnolia makes leaves first, and only at the end of spring, after any frost has past, does it show a magnificent display of flowers. They have 9–12 cream to snow-white slightly crumpled tepals, with a conspicuous

Magnolia 'Charles Coates'
STEPHEN LYUS

centre of purple-red stamens. When fully opened they are up to 18cm wide and unlike one of its parents (*M. tripetala*) they have a lovely lemon scented fragrance. However, the flowers are short-lived, seldom produced in abundance and discolour within a day during inclement weather.

The leaves are up to 35cm long, ovate, bright to deep green with a pale underneath, and are clustered at the shoot tips.

Magnolia liliiflora 'Nigra'

LABELLED: *Magnolia quinquepeta* 'Nigra'
SYNONYMS: Woody Orchid, Lily-Flowered Magnolia
PREFERRED SITUATION: Full/semi sun; well draining deep soil

M. liliiflora was introduced to Britain from Japan in 1790, but is probably native to China although it is not known in the wild.

It makes a large deciduous multi-branched shrub or small tree. The pinkish purple upright flowers have a pleasant fragrance similar to sweet lemons. It begins to flower in mid-spring as the leaves start to emerge and continues for two months, although it is not so effective when the foliage obscures the flowers. 'Nigra' is assumed to be the cultivar most widely grown, but much confusion exists regarding the identity of the true plant.

Magnolia liliiflora 'Nigra'
STEPHEN LYUS

MOUNT CONGREVE, WATERFORD, EIRE
Rhododendron lindleyi

PREFERRED SITUATION: well-drained sandy loam soil; protected from frost but avoid full shade, as it tends to make the plants less hardy.

R. lindleyi is one of the Maddenia species and is native to Nepal, S.E. Tibet and Manipur where it is usually epiphytic in trees and on cliffs. It is easy to grow from seed or cuttings and blooms when quite young. The growth habit is unusual, with an open style without many branches. It wants to produce stems from the ground with few side branches. This generally earns it a pejorative description such as 'straggly' or 'leggy'. It can grow up to 4.5m tall.

It has large trumpet-shaped flowers, up to 10cm long, in trusses usually of three to seven that are white often tinged with pink and with a wonderfully strong, sweet-spicy fragrance.

Rhododendron lindleyi
STEPHEN LYUS

Contributions by Andy Simons, Mike Robinson and Steve Lyus

Exceptional new hybrids 2007

A steady stream of new rhododendron hybrids are named or registered every year, mainly by breeders in the USA and Europe and although it is becoming increasingly difficult to separate the best from the ordinary, there are always a few which seem particularly promising. Bearing in mind that it takes at least 10 years for the results of a cross to be evaluated and another few years before the variety can be made available, we thought it might be interesting to provide a regular 'preview' of those plants which we expect to be introduced in the near future.

R. 'Wild Ginger'

('Apricot Fantasy' x 'Hill's Low Red')
Perfect ball-shaped trusses of about 20 broadly funnel-shaped wavy-edged flowers in pale yellowish orange, shading to a lighter pale yellow towards the lobe edges and darkening towards the throat. The reverse of the flower is a pale orange-yellow blending to light yellow and with deep pink streaking on the midribs. Forms a low-growing, compact shrub with neat dark-green foliage and strong-red buds. A very promising new hybrid from Jim Barlup which flowers in late May.

R. 'Show Girl'

('Nancy Evans' x 'Senator Henry Jackson')
A very attractive new hybrid by Cameron Fleming, one of the UK's few active hybridisers. Masses of waxy, pure lemon-yellow flowers on a sturdy, rounded shrub. Best in Class at SRS Oban Show. Flowers in May

R. 'Wild Ginger'
GERALD DIXON

R. 'Show Girl'
CAMERON FLEMING

R. 'Web's Bee'

(*yakushimanum* x *proteoides*)
A very compact low-growing shrub, very much like *Rhododendron proteoides* in foliage and habit but very free-flowering with well-filled trusses of pale-pink medium-sized flowers in May. Surprisingly easy to please. A relatively unknown hybrid from the late Warren Berg, only grown in a couple of Danish gardens and, more recently, by Hachmann.

R. 'Pure Luxury'

('Soulkew' x 'Elizabeth de Rothschild')
Beautifully poised, lax trusses of up to 10 six-lobed funnel-shaped flowers of heavy, silky consistency, in creamy-white with deeper yellow shading on the upper lobe and with two red basal rays. The lower lobes are flat, the upper 3 lobes recurved to give a lily-like effect. Sweetly scented, an upright close-growing shrub with attractive light-green foliage. Very free-flowering over a long period in May. A new hybrid, raised and introduced by Brooklands Nurseries.

R. 'Web's Bee'
GERALD DIXON

R. 'Pure Luxury'
GERALD DIXON

Contribution by Gerald Dixon

Awards to plants 2006/2007

Magnolias

***Magnolia campbellii* 'Dick Banks'**
was awarded an AM in November 2006.
The same cross as *Magnolia campbellii* Raffellii Group,
this plant was given to Richard Banks by Harold Hillier
as a seedling in 1973. It first
flowered in April 1991 and
by 1995 had attained a
height of 13m and a girth of
about 1m. Growing in Park
Wood at Hergest, it usually
flowers in late March or early
April and tends to bloom
best every second year. The
large flowers, about 20cm in
diameter, are white inside
suffused with bluish pink
with deeper-coloured streaks near the margins. The
outer surface is deeper coloured and slightly paler
towards the centre.

M. campbellii 'Dick Banks'
ELIZABETH BANKS

Rhododendrons

***Rhododendron* 'Concorde'**
(*yakushimanum* x 'The Master')
was awarded an AM at Chelsea 2006.
Hybridised and raised by Arthur
George of Hydon Nurseries in 1966,
this is somewhat taller growing than
most yak hybrids, to about 6–8ft,
with light green leaves and large
trusses of fine white flowers with a
pronounced green blotch – completely hardy, with great substance
and flowering in early June.

R. 'Concorde'
RHS

In May 2007 the RHS Rhododendron & Camellia Committee visited the Royal Botanic Garden in Edinburgh and made awards to six species of vireya rhododendrons held in its collection. These represent the first vireyas to gain awards since 1981. Their varietal names have now been registered.

Rhododendron gardenia Schltr.
'Jennifer Jean' AM 19769192
A slow growing large plant which has flowered regularly since attaining about 1m in height. It is named after the genus *Gardenia* noted for its strongly perfumed flowers and it is well named as the large fleshy flowers fill the greenhouse with scent when open and the plant always elicits comment from visitors when in bloom. It is named after the daughter of the collector who is a passionate environmentalist and field worker in the tropics.

Rhododendron loranthiflorum Sleumer
'Dick Shaw' AM 19839161
This species has been in cultivation since 1964 and was introduced to Britain from Australia in 1983. It performs well wherever vireyas thrive and there have been glowing reports of its performance in Australia, New Zealand and the USA. The plants cover themselves in the white slightly scented flowers at least once a year, usually in spring in Edinburgh. It is named after Richard (Dick) Shaw, formerly assistant curator at the Benmore Botanic Garden, then curator at Kew and finally Edinburgh. Dick was a fiery character who took a lively interest in the Vireya Collection and scientific collections in general when he was in charge.

Members of the Rhododendron & Camellia Committee at work at the RBG Edinburgh
ANDY SIMONS

R. gardenia 'Jennifer Jean'
LYNSEY MUIR

R. loranthiflorum 'Dick Shaw'
LYNSEY MUIR

Rhododendron macgregoriae F. Muell.
'Paddy Woods' AM 19688041
This collection has been growing for almost 40 years in the Royal Botanic Garden Edinburgh. It flowers freely, covering itself in bright yellow flowers in the spring and often flowering well at other times of the year. This is one of the easiest species to grow and, coming from relatively low altitudes, is heat tolerant. In the wild this species is very widespread in New Guinea and very variable in flower colour. This cultivar is a good clear yellow with the flowers produced well clear of the leaves. It is named after Patrick Woods the collector, botanist and horticulturist at the Royal Botanic Garden Edinburgh. He went on several expeditions to SE Asia collecting plants, took a great interest and published on rhododendrons and orchids.

R. macgregoriae 'Paddy Woods'
LYNSEY MUIR

Rhododendron macgregoriae F. Muell.
'Tom Grieve' AM 19875242
This clone has light orange, almost bronze flowers which are very freely produced mostly in the spring. It is named after Thomas Grieve, a dedicated plantsman who worked in South America for much of his life but returned to Britain as a gardener at the Royal Botanic Garden Edinburgh. He was in charge of the Vireya Collection for a number of years and was the first person to persuade *Rhododendron saxifragoides* to flower.

R. macgregoriae 'Tom Grieve'
LYNSEY MUIR

Rhododendron polyanthemum Sleumer
'Sheila Collenette' FCC 19799207
Flowering just once a year, this species puts on an immense display of bright orange, scented flowers in the late spring. Surprisingly, this species was not described until 1963 despite now being common on Mt Kinabalu in Sabah. This cultivar is named in honour of the original collector of the species who made a significant contribution to the know-ledge of vireyas in Sabah and has more recently published a classic work on the flowers of Saudi Arabia.

Rhododendron rousei Argent
'John Rouse' PC 19905026
This species is now grown in collections worldwide and invariably gets favourable comment from growers. The lustrous dark green leaves contrast with the pure white of the flowers which in Edinburgh are often best produced in the gloom of November or December. It was introduced from Sibuyan Island in the Philippines, its only known locality in 1989. It lacks scent but will flower two or three times a year if deadheaded. Both species and clone are named after Dr John Rouse of Melbourne, Australia, eminent scientist and grower and hybridiser of vireyas.

Contributions by Lawrence Banks, Anne George and George Argent

R. polyanthemum 'Sheila Collenette'
LYNSEY MUIR

R. rousei Argent 'John Rouse'
LYNSEY MUIR

Challenge Cup Winners 2007

ALAN HARDY CHALLENGE SALVER

Awarded at the Early Rhododendron Competition to the exhibitor attaining the most points.
Mr John Anderson, Exbury Gardens

Three of the winning exhibits that contributed to the award (see also *Rhododendron glischroides*, page 133)

Rhododendron macabeanum
MICHAEL SHUTTLEWORTH

Rhododendron 'Kalimna'
MICHAEL SHUTTLEWORTH

Rhododendron ririei
MICHAEL SHUTTLEWORTH

THE McLAREN CHALLENGE CUP

The best exhibit of any species of rhododendron, one truss shown in Class 3 of the Main Rhododendron Competition.
Mr. Brian Wright, Crowborough

Rhododendron bureavii

Rhododendron bureavii
TIMOTHY SWAN

THE ROZA STEVENSON CHALLENGE CUP

The best exhibit of any species of rhododendron, one spray or branch with one or more than one truss shown in Class 4 of the Main Rhododendron Competition
Mr John Anderson,
Exbury Gardens

Rhododendron oreodoxa var. *fargesii*

Rhododendron oreodoxa var. *fargesii*   GEORGE HARGREAVES

THE LODER CHALLENGE CUP

The best exhibit of any hybrid rhododendron, one truss shown in Class 33 of the Main Rhododendron Competition
Mr John Anderson,
Exbury Gardens

Rhododendron 'Fortune'

Rhododendron 'Fortune'   GEORGE HARGREAVES

THE CROSFIELD CHALLENGE CUP

The best exhibit of three rhododendrons raised by or in the garden of the exhibitor, one truss of each, shown in Class 35 of the Main Rhododendron Competition
Mr John Anderson,
Exbury Gardens

Rhododendron 'Lionel's Triumph'
Rhododendron 'Edmund de Rothschild'
Rhododendron 'Janet'

Rhododendron 'Lionel's Triumph'   GEORGE HARGREAVES

LEONARDSLEE BOWL

The best exhibit of twelve cultivars of camellias, one bloom of each shown in Class 10 of the Main Camellia Competition
Mr Andrew Simons

Camellias:
'Bravo'
'Desire'
'Dr Clifford Parks'
'Harold L Paige'
'Kick Off'
'Lila Naff'
'Moonlight Bay'
'Nuccio's Carousel'
'Pavlova'
'Pink Dahlia'
'Valentine's Day'
'Wildfire'

ANDY SIMONS

BEST IN SHOW (SE Branch Show at Borde Hill)

Mr Ed Ikin, Nymans

Rhododendron schlippenbachii

Rhododendron schlippenbachii   MICHAEL SHUTTLEWORTH

RHS Rhododendron & Camellia Committee

CHAIRMAN
DR M L A ROBINSON Hindleap Lodge, Priory Road, Forest Row, East Sussex RH18 5JF
Tel: 01342 822745 Email: mlarob@hotmail.com

VICE CHAIRMAN
Vacancy

SECRETARY
DR D EDWARDS RHS Garden Wisley, Woking, Surrey GU23 6QB
Email: dawnedwards@rhs.org.uk

MEMBERS

MR P D EVANS West Netherton, Drewsteignton, Devon EX6 6RB
Tel/Fax: 01647 281285 (phone first) Email: philip.d.evans@talk21.com

MR M FLANAGAN Verderers, Wick Road, Englefield Green, Egham, Surrey TW20 0HL
Email: mark.flanagan@theroyallandscape.co.uk

MR M C FOSTER White House Farm, Ivy Hatch, Sevenoaks, Kent TN15 0NN
Email: rosifoster@aol.com

MR J T GALLAGHER Oldfield, 29 Moorlands Road, Verwood, Dorset BH31 7PD
Email: magnolianut@hotmail.com

MR A F GEORGE Hydon Nurseries, Hydon Heath, Godalming, Surrey GU8 4AZ

MR J G HILLIER VMH c/o Hillier Nurseries Ltd, Ampfield House, Ampfield, Romsey, Hampshire SO51 9PA
Email: john_hillier@hillier.co.uk

DR R H L JACK Edgemoor, Loch Road, Lanark ML11 9BG

MR T METHUEN-CAMPBELL Penrice Castle, Reynoldston, Swansea, West Glamorgan SA3 1LN

MR D G MILLAIS Millais Nurseries, Crosswater Farm, Churt, Farnham, Surrey GU10 2JN
Email: sales@rhododendrons.co.uk

MR M PHAROAH Lower Tithe Barn, Marwood, Barnstaple, Devon EX31 4EB
Email: malcolmpharoah@supanet.com

MR A W SIMONS Wingfield House, 11 Brinsmade Road, Ampthill, Bedfordshire MK45 2PP
Email: a.simons@ntlworld.com

MR A V SKINNER MBE 2 Frog Firle Cottage, Alfriston, nr Polegate, East Sussex BN26 5TT

MR M O SLOCOCK VMH Hillside Cottage, Brentmoor Road, West End, Woking, Surrey GU24 9ND

MR C B TOMLIN Starborough Nursery, Starborough Road, Marsh Green, Edenbridge, Kent TN8 5RB

MISS J TREHANE 353 Church Cottages, Hampreston, Wimborne, Dorset BH21 7LX
Email: jennifer@trehane.co.uk

MR C H WILLIAMS Burncoose Nurseries, Gwennap, Redruth, Cornwall TR16 6BJ
Email: diana@burncoose.co.uk

Rhododendron, Camellia & Magnolia Group

OFFICERS

CHAIRMAN
DR MIKE L A ROBINSON Hindleap Lodge, Priory Road, Forest Row, East Sussex RH18 5JF
Tel: 01342 822745 Email: mlarob@hotmail.com

VICE CHAIRMAN
MR PHILIP D EVANS West Netherton, Drewsteignton, Devon EX6 6RB
Tel/Fax: 01647 281285 (phone first) Email: philip.d.evans@talk21.com

HON. TREASURER
MR MARTIN D C GATES 12 Marlborough Road, Chandlers Ford, Eastleigh, Hampshire SO53 5DH
Tel: 023 8025 2843

HON. SECRETARY
MRS PAT BUCKNELL Botallick, Lanreath, Looe, Cornwall PL13 2PF
Tel: 01503 220215 Email: patbucknell@btinternet.com

HON. MEMBERSHIP SECRETARY
MR RUPERT L C ELEY East Bergholt Place, East Bergholt, Suffolk CO7 6UP
Tel: 01206 299224 Fax: 01206 299229 Email: sales@placeforplants.co.uk

HON. YEARBOOK EDITOR & ARCHIVIST
PAM HAYWARD Woodtown, Sampford Spiney, Yelverton, Devon PL20 6LJ
Tel/Fax: 01822 852122 Email: pam@woodtown.net

HON. BULLETIN EDITOR
MR JOHN RAWLING The Spinney, Station Road, Woldingham, Surrey CR3 7DD
Tel: 01883 653341 Email: jr.eye@virgin.net

HON. TOURS ORGANISER
MRS JUDY HALLETT The Old Rectory, Thruxton, Herefordshire HR2 9AX
Tel: 01981 570401 Email: judy.hallett@googlemail.com

WEBMASTER
MR GRAHAM MILLS Tregoning Mill, St. Keverne, Helston, Cornwall TR12 6QE
Tel: 01326 280382 Fax: 0871 433 7066 Email: graham@tregoningmill.co.uk

COMMITTEE MEMBERS

MR ERIC ANNAL 36 Hillview Crescent, Edinburgh EH12 8QG
Tel: 0131 334 2574 Email: eric.annal@btinternet.com

MR JOHN D HARSANT Newton House, Well Lane, Heswall, Wirral CH60 8NF
Tel: 0151 342 3664 Fax: 0151 348 4015 Email: john@harsant.uk.com (Publicity Officer)

MR STEPHEN LYUS 13 Manor Drive, Surbiton, Surrey KT5 8NE
Tel: 0208 399 4122 Email: slyus@yahoo.co.uk

MR ANDY SIMONS Wingfield House, 11 Brinsmade Road, Ampthill, Bedfordshire MK45 2PP
Tel: 01525 753398 Email: a.simons@ntlworld.com

MR ALASTAIR T STEVENSON Appledore, Upton Bishop, Ross-on-Wye, Herefordshire HR9 7UL
Tel: 01989 780285 Fax: 01989 780591 Email: alastairstevenson@MPAconsulting.co.uk
(Co-ordinator of Events and Stationery Officer)

MR IVOR T STOKES Llyshendy, Llandeilo, Carmarthenshire SA19 6YA
Tel/Fax: 01558 823233 Email: ivor.t.stokes@btopenworld.com

MR BRIAN E WRIGHT Kilsaran, Fielden Lane, Crowborough, Sussex TN6 1TL
Tel: 01892 653207 Fax: 01892 669550 Email: iriswright@msn.com

BRANCH CHAIRMEN

INTERNATIONAL
MRS MIRANDA GUNN Ramster, Chiddingfold, Surrey GU8 4SN
Tel: 01428 644422 Email: miranda@ramsterweddings.co.uk

NEW FOREST
Vacancy

NORFOLK
Vacancy

NORTH WALES/NORTHWEST
MR C E J BRABIN Rosewood, Puddington Village, Neston CH64 5SS
Tel: 0151 353 1193 Email: angela.brabin@tesco.net

PEAK
DR DAVID R IVES 18 Park Road, Birstall, Leicestershire LE4 3AU
Tel: 0116 2675118 Email: rosiedavid.ives@btopenworld.com

SOUTHEAST
MR BARRY HASELTINE Goodwins, Snow Hill, Crawley Down, Sussex RH10 3EF
Tel: 01342 713132 Email: barry.haseltine@which.net

SOUTHWEST
MR COLIN H T BROWN West Winds, Lustleigh, Newton Abbot, Devon TQ13 9TR
Tel: 01647 277268 Email: marylou@lustleigh.plus.com

ULSTER
MR PATRICK FORDE Seaforde, Downpatrick, Co. Down BT30 8PG
Tel: 028 4481 1225 Fax: 028 4481 1370 Email: Plants@SeafordeGardens.com

WESSEX
MRS MIRANDA GUNN Ramster, Chiddingfold, Surrey GU8 4SN
Tel: 01428 644422 Fax: 01428 658345 Email: miranda@ramsterweddings.co.uk

CONVENOR OF GROUP SEED BANK

MR GERALD J DIXON Brooklands, Shute, Axminster, Devon, EX13 7QF
Tel: 01404 831689 Email: brooklandrhododendrons@btinternet.com

WEBSITE

www.rhodogroup-rhs.org

Index

Camellia

'Beni Hassaku' 106
'Bravo' 126
'Browncreek's Carmen' 4, 106
'Browncreek's Chiffon' 106
'Browncreek's Delight' 105
'Browncreek's Gem', 106
'Browncreek's Harlequin' 106
'Browncreek's Lustre' 106
'Browncreek's Moonbeam' 106
'Browncreek's Pageantry' 106
'Browncreek's Purity' 106
'Browncreek's Sunrise' 106
'Browncreek's Sunset', 106
'Browncreek's Sweetness' 106
'Browncreek's Twilight' 106
'Buffy's Beauty' 106
'Clarissa' 106
'Coral Queen' 106
cuspidata 24
'Daintiness' 106
'Deep Scarlet' 114
'Deep Secret' 114
'Desire' 126
'Dr Clifford Parks' 126
'Elizabeth de Rothschild' 105
'Golden Spangles' 105
'Harold L Paige' 126
japonica 7, 26, 27, 28, 31, 104, 106
  'Korean Fire' 30
  'Longwood Centennial' 31
  'Rogetsu' 106
  'Sylva' 106
  'Wildfire' 106
'J.C. Williams' 105
'Jury's Yellow' 106
'Kick Off' 126
'Korean Fire' 31
'Longwood Valentine' 31
'Lila Naff' 126
'Mattie Cole' 106
'Moonlight Bay' 126
'Nuccio's Carousel' 114, 126
'Nuccio's Ruby' 113
'Pavlova' 126
'Philippa Forward' 105

'Pink Dahlia' 113, 126
'Robert Strauss' 106
reticulata 106, 113, 114
saluenensis 113
'Salutation' 106
sasanqua 106
'Spring Festival' 113
transnokoensis 113
'Valentine's Day' 126
'Wildfire' 126
x *williamsii* 104, 105
  'Donation' 38
  'Mary Jobson' 105

Magnolia

acuminata 92, 116
campbellii 36, 94
  'Dick Banks' 120
  ssp. mollicomata 41
  Raffellii Group, 120
cathcartii 96
cavaleriei 83, 84, 85, 94
chapensis 93, 94
'Charles Coates' 116
coco 81
compressa 96
conifera 88, 89
  var. *chingii* 88, 89, 94, 95
crassipes 93, 94, 96
dandyi 90
'Daphne' 116
dawsoniana 7, 21, 24, 50, 51, 53, 54, 55
delavayi 38, 41, 81
dianica 87, 94
doltsopa 94, 95, 96
duclouxii 94, 96
ernestii 93, 94, 95, 96
figo 94, 96
floribunda 93
x *foggii* 95
  'Allspice' 95
fordiana 90, 91, 94, 96
foveolata 84, 85, 86, 89, 93, 94, 95
  var. *cinerascens* 85

fulva 93
grandiflora 81, 85, 87, 89, 91
insignis 87, 88, 89, 93, 94, 96
kobus 96
laevifolia 86, 93, 94, 95, 96
  'Michelle' 86
  'Velvet and Cream' 96
lanuginosa 93, 94
liliiflora 117
  'Nigra' 117
x *loebneri* 92
'Lois' 116
lotungensis 91, 92, 93, 94, 95
macclurei 83, 93, 94, 95, 96
martinii 94, 95
maudiae 82, 83, 84, 92, 93, 94, 95, 96
megaphylla 90, 93
moto 89, 90, 94
'Nimbus' 94
nitida 81, 91, 92, 95
odora 93, 95
omeiensis 92, 93
ovoidea 93
platypetala 83, 84, 94
quinquepeta
  'Nigra' 117
'Royal Alma' 6
rufibarbata 90
salicifolia 38
sargentiana 7, 50, 51, 53, 54, 55, 56, 57
  var. *robusta* 24
shiluensis 93
sieboldii 89
sinica 93
skinneriana 94, 96
x *soulangeana* 38
sprengeri 24
  var. *diva* 24
tripetala 117
virginiana 83
wilsonii 24
yuyuanensis 90, 91, 92, 94, 95
zenii 83

Rhododendron

aberconwayi 12
  'Earl Lloyd George' 12, 13
'Addy Wery' 59
adinophyllum 100, 102
'Adrian Koster' 33
ambiguum 9
anthopogon 102
'Arctic Fox' 60
'Arena' 34
argyrophyllum 56
arboreum 109
  subsp. *nilagiricum* 67
  subsp. *zeylanicum* 66, 67, 107
argipeplum 109
atjehense 100
augustinii 9, 100
auriculatum 67
'Avon' 34
balangense 20, 110
bhutanense 110
'Beaver' 60
'Beau Brummel' 33
'Beefeater' 33, 34
'Beta' 42
'Billy Budd' 34
'Biscuit Box' 34
'Bulldog' 42
'Burma Road' 33, 34
'Brenda's Choice' 10, 11
bureavii 124
bureavioides 110
'Calder' 34
calophytum 24, 56
  var. *openshawianum* 15
'Cam' 34
capitatum 17
Carmen Group 10
carolinianum 10
Cartonii Group 13
cerasinum 110
cinnabarinum 10, 109
'Cherubim' 42
'Cherwell' 34
'Chikor' 59
'Clyde' 34
'Concorde' 120
'Constable' 34
'Coral Island' 34

'Coral Reef' 34
'Cornish Cream' 42
'Cornish Glow' 42
'Crater's Edge' 110
crenulatum 102
'Curlew' 59
'Dart' 34
davidsonianum 24
'Deben' 34
decorum
  subsp. *cordatum* 57
'Dee' 34
'Degas' 34
'Derwent' 34
'Deveron' 34
'Diamant' 60
'Diamant White' 61
dichroanthum 11, 33
'Ding Dong' 37, 42
'Douggie Betteridge' 115
'Drapa' 60
'Eddystone' 34
edgeworthii 107
'Edmund de Rothschild' 125
elegantulum 98
'El Greco' 34
Elizabeth Group 10
elliottii 33
'Emerald Isle' 34
eriogynum 33
'Everest' 60
'Evita' 60
'Fabia' 33
Fabia Group 9, 11
facetum 114
'Fal' 34
faucium 110
flinckii 110
'Fortune' 125
fortunei 10, 115
'Fragrantissimum' 37
'Frome' 34
'Fusilier' 33
galactinum 20
gardenia
  'Jennifer Jean' 121
'Glenda Gough' 12
Glendoick® Crimson 60
Glendoick® Drea 60

Glendoick® Garnet 60
Glendoick® Glacie 60
Glendoick® Goblin 60
Glendoick® Rosebud 61
Glendoick® Snowflakes 61
giganteum 67
'Ginny Gee' 109
glischroides 124, 133
'Gloriana' 34
'Golden Oriole' 37
'Golfer' 109
grande 109
griersonianum 10, 11
griffithianum 67, 109
'Hanger's Flame' 34
'Hatsuguri' 59
hodgsonii 107, 110
'Holiad Michelle' 10
'Holiad Blush' 11
'Holiad Brenda' 10
'Holiad Caroline Llewellyn'
  11, 12
'Holiad Glenda Gough' 11
'Holiad Strawberry Ripple', 11
'Holiad Trevor' 9
'Holiad Yellow Beauty 11
huidongense 57, 58
'Humber' 34
Hybridum Group 13
'Janet' 125
'Johanna' 60
'Johnnie Johnston' 39, 42
'June Bee' 108, 109
'Kalimna' 124
keiskei 108
'Kensey' 34
'Kermesina' 60
kesangiae 110
kiusianum 60
'Koichiro Wada' 33
'Koromo Shikibu' 60, 61
'Lady Bowes Lyon' 33, 34
'Lady Digby' 114, 115
'Laerdal' 42
'Lal Kapra' 42
'Lanyon' 42
'Lascaux' 34
'Lemur' 59, 60
'Liffey' 34

lindleyi 117
'Lionel's Triumph' 125
litiense 33
Loderi 'King George' 37, 114
Loderi 'Pink Diamond' 114
loranthiflorum
  'Dick Shaw' 121
'Lord Rudolph' 115
lutescens 24
macabeanum 41, 97, 107, 124
macgregoriae
  'Paddy Woods' 122
  'Tom Grieve' 122
mallotum 107
'Marushka' 60
'May Day' 10
'Medway' 34
'Mersey' 34
'Miss Pink' 42
'Moonshine' 34
'Moonshine Bright' 34
'Moonshine Crescent' 34
'Moonshine Glow' 34
'Moonshine Supreme' 34
morii 97
'Morvah' 38, 39, 40, 42
moupinense 24
'Mrs EC Stirling' 78
'Mucronatum' 60
mucronulatum 109
nakaharae 60
'Nanceglos' 42
'Naomi' 33
'Nene' 34
'New Comet' 34
nivale
  ssp *boreale* 19
ochraceum 56
oreodoxa 21, 56
  var. *fargesii* 125
'Orwell' 34
pachysanthum
  'Pachy Bee' 108
pachytrichum 56, 115
'Patty Bee' 109

'Palestrina' 59
'Panda' 60
'Penalverne' 42
'Penhale' 42
'Perfect Lady' 34
'Petia' 34
phaeochrysum 110
'Pilgrim' 33
'Pink Ghost' 34
'Planetum' 10
polyanthemum
  'Sheila Collenette' 123
ponticum 37
principis 110
pronum 107
proteoides 107, 108, 110
przewalskii 16
'Ptarmigan' 59
'Pure Luxury' 119
'Raspberry Ripple' 34
'Red Red' 60
'Renoir' 33, 34
rex
  subsp. *rex* 53, 56, 57
'Ribble' 34
ririei 124
'Romany Chal' 33
rousei 'John Rouse' 123
roxieanum 110
'Royal Blood' 34
'Rubeotinctum' 42
rubiginosum 56
rufu 21
russatum 97
scabrifolium
  var. *spiciferum* 10
schlippenbachii 126
selense 9, 11
'Serena' 34
'Severn' 34
'Shepherd's Morning' 34
'Show Girl' 118
sinogrande 37, 107, 115
'Sir F Moore' 33
souliei 16

'Squirrel' 60
'Stour' 34
strigillosum 114, 115
subansiriense 107
sulfureum 97
sumatranum 102
sutchuenense 10, 24
'Tamar' 34
'Tay' 34
'Taurus' 115
'Tees' 34
'Telstar' 34
'Temple Belle' 37
'Tensing' 33, 34
'Tequila Sunrise' 33, 34
'Thames' 34
thomsonii 109
'Too Bee' 109
'Tosca' 34
'Trent' 34
'Tweed' 34
'Tyne' 34
uvariifolium 110
vanderbiltianum 100, 102
'Wansbeck' 34
wardii 10, 97, 110
watsonii 21
'Waveney' 34
'Web's Bee' 119
'Wee Bee' 109
'Weybridge' 34
weyrichii 109
'Wild Ginger' 118
wiltonii 15
'Windrush' 34
'Wisley Blush' 34
'Wisley Pearl' 34
'Wombat' 60
'Woodcock' 34
'Wye' 34
'Yaku Fairy', 108
yakushimanum 33, 34
yedoense
  var. *poukhanense* 109

RHODODENDRON GLISCHROIDES'
MICHAEL SHUTTLEWORTH

The Rothschild Collection

Exbury remains very much a family Garden, home to the Rothschild Collection of rhododendrons, azaleas, camellias, rare trees and plants.

Created by Lionel de Rothschild in the 1920's, the gardens offer over 200 acres of natural beauty and variety that echo to the names of the famous plant hunters – Kingdon-Ward, Forrest and Wilson.

The early spring Rock Garden and Heather Garden, daffodils, camellias, magnolias and primroses give way to bluebells, rhododendrons and azaleas, with colour and birdsong every turn. The summer months bring cool and shady riverside walks, hydrangeas and showpiece exotic and herbaceous gardens. Autumn arrives in a blaze of colour from waterside maples, sweet gums and dogwoods. See Exbury's National Collection of Nyssa and Oxydendrum, and be dazzled by the collection of nerines in the Five Arrows Gallery.

Sister attraction "Maize Maze" open July – September. Separate charge.

EXBURY
——— GARDENS ———
& STEAM RAILWAY

THE NEW FOREST
relax · explore · enjoy

thenewforest.co.uk

Plant Centre; Gift Shop; Mr Eddy's Restaurant and Tearooms; Steam Railway; Buggy Tours. "Meet and Greet", guided walks and tailored talks can be arranged on request.

General enquiries: (023) 8089 1203; 24 hr info line: (023) 8089 9422 Plant Centre:(023) 8089 8625; Mr Eddy's Restaurant and Tearooms: (023) 8089 8737

www.exbury.co.uk or e-mail: nigel.philpott@exbury.co.uk

Exbury Gardens in the New Forest, SO45 1AZ, 20 mins from Junction 2, M27 West.

The Savill Garden

England's finest woodland garden

From late winter the woodlands are filled with magnolias, rhododendrons, camellias and many other wonderful plants.

Plus plant sales, shopping and terraced restaurant in our award winning Savill Building.

Open daily 10am–4:30pm (Nov–Feb), 10am–6pm (Mar–Oct)

The Savill Garden, Wick Lane, Englefield Green, Surrey TW20 0UU

Located off A30, M25 Junction 13 or M4 Junction 6

Tel 01784 435544
enquiries@theroyallandscape.co.uk